Nasty Norwich

The whole gory story!

TREVOR HEATON

Illustrated by
Holly James
cover illustration Tony Hall

BOSWORTH
BOOKS

Published by Bosworth Books,

Rose End, High Street, Whissonsett, Dereham, Norfolk NR20 5AP

First published in the UK by Bosworth Books 2005

Text and design copyright Trevor Heaton, 2005

Cover illustration copyright Tony Hall, 2005

All other illustrations copyright Holly James, 2005

Educational consultants: Julie Dicks BA (Hons), PGCE

and Velma Heaton BA (Hons), PGCE

ISBN 0-9551153-0-2 (978-0-9551153-0-1)

Printed and bound by Biddles Ltd, 24 Rollesby Road, Hardwick Industrial Estate,

King's Lynn, Norfolk PE30 4LS

NO HISTORY TEACHERS WERE INJURED DURING THE MAKING OF THIS BOOK

Contents

Introduction

'Norwich – a fine city' say the road signs. And so it is: an historic city full of interesting little streets, beautiful buildings and nice people. Sounds lovely, doesn't it?

Yes, but look back in the past and you'll see that before we ended up with Fine Norwich we had Rebellious Norwich, Violent Norwich, Blitzed Norwich, Disease-ridden Norwich and, for hundreds of years, Very, *Very* Smelly Norwich.

Let's go back in time and meet the people who made it that way... if you've got the stomach for it.

Ladies and gentlemen, welcome to NASTY NORWICH!

The Start!

Meet the Ugs

These are the Ug family. Say hello.

They are special because they are the first inhabitants of Norwich. Nice, aren't they? They lived near the Wensum in the city perhaps 35,000 years ago. The Ugs needed to make tools for hunting and slicing up furry things.

This was thousands of years before Man discovered how to use metal, so instead he used flint. By hitting flint in a certain way you can end up with a nice sharp axe or arrowhead.

Good news for Ug, Mrs Ug and all the little Ug-lettes.

Bad news for the local wildlife!

A chip off the old block

We know what Ug was up to because when you make flint tools you leave an awful lot of waste chippings behind called flakes. Archaeologists have found these axes and flakes around the Carrow area on what would have been a sand island in the Wensum thousands of years ago.

The most recent finds were made during construction of the new stand at Norwich City FC.

Happily for Ug and all his descendants, chased around the Wensum valley by angry wildlife for thousands of years, archaeologists discovered in 1985 in a dig at Fishergate that there was a big thick layer of peat – a substance made from rotting plants. So our hunters would have been able to find plenty of trees to hide in! Let's leave Ug's descendants up that tree and fast-forward several thousand years to Norwich's next big step.

The Roamin' Romans

Nice Country. Let's Invade it.

AD43. The Romans wade ashore in Kent. The Emperor Claudius has had his legions invade these mysterious islands in pursuit of glory – and gold too, naturally.

The Romans are smart. They wouldn't have conquered so many lands if they weren't. They know a really easy way to conquer Britain is to make friends with as many of the native tribes as they can. Divide and rule – it's the oldest trick in the book. Cunning Claudius!

Icky Iceni

One of the most powerful tribes was the Iceni, who lived in Norfolk, Suffolk and part of what is now Cambridgeshire. Under Boudica they revolted against the hated Romans in AD60-61. A huge Iceni army swept down through East Anglia, completely splatting the new Roman

'I told you not to make fun of their accent!'

towns of Camulodunum (Colchester), Verulamium (St Albans) and Londonium, and beating up Romans left, right and centre – until they came up against the Roman general Suetonius Paulinus. Ouch.

Result: Romans 1, Iceni 0.

So where does this tie in with Norwich?

Well, after the revolt, the Romans tried to encourage the Iceni to become more civilised (= more like the Romans). One of their top ways for doing this was to build towns.

And so Venta Icenorum was born.

Flop city

The only trouble was: *it didn't work*. If it had done, there probably wouldn't have been a Norwich because we'd have all been living in Caistor St Edmund instead. Big cities like Manchester, Leicester and London all evolved from successful Roman towns.

But the Romans weren't to know this. So they went ahead and founded Venta Icenorum ('the market place of the Iceni') at Caistor St Edmund, a few miles south of present-day Norwich. However, it never really caught on – only a small part was ever built on, and when the market place burned down it was not replaced for 50 years!

Meanwhile, over at the Wensum...

All this activity at Venta doesn't mean the Romans weren't around in what was to become Norwich. Being able to steer ships right up the river was a handy method of transport – and the Roman coastline was much closer to Norwich than it is today.

But just how much Roman activity there was is a mystery.

Here's the problem: Every new set of residents of a town builds on the remains of the previous buildings.

In an ancient city like Norwich this has happened over and over again. That means the Roman archaeology might well be there but buried under layer after layer of other things.

But we do have a few clues...

Crossroads and coffins

Archaeologists have looked at the ancient street plan of Norwich in detail and reckon there could have been two roads running through the area in Roman times.

One, running east to west, might have run along Dereham Road through St Benedict's, under the nave of the Cathedral, through Pilling Park and along to Brundall.

The second possibly ran north-south along Long John Hill, Ber Street and Oak Street.

In 1974 and 1987 Roman pottery was discovered near Magdalen Street, and in 1861 what appeared to have been Roman lead coffins were found off Dereham Road. Which would have made them the dead centre of Roman Norwich, presumably*.

And do you know, in a funny sort of way Venta Icenorum did turn into Norwich.

Well, part of it – historians believe Roman tiles found among the stones of Norwich Cathedral were carted over from Caistor as building material.

(* A joke probably nearly as old as the Romans!)

The Stinky Saxons

It's Getting Dark

It's AD 410 and things aren't going very well with the Roman Empire. Already split into two parts – East and West – it's attacked by land and sea by tribes pushing westward and south. Even Rome itself is under threat, so in desperation Emperor Honorius orders the last Roman legions to withdraw from Britain.

'Sorry lads,' he tells the Britons, 'You're on your own.'

'Oh, wonderful,' say the Brits.

The Dark Ages have begun...

Say hello to the Saxons

Now here's a strange thing. The Romans built lots of forts (like Brancaster) to try to keep the Saxons out – but ended up recruiting them as hired soldiers to fight other Saxons!

Surprise, surprise – these Saxons decided they rather liked the look of Norfolk and wanted to stay.

Where did they live?

The Anglo-Saxons had no use for towns at first, so although they probably had a few villages near Venta Icenorum they must have let the town's buildings fall to ruin.

It's thought there must have been some living in Norwich, because in 1898 a cremated early Saxon was discovered at Eade Road. Perhaps they lived in some mud-and-thatched huts near the Wensum.

But it's still not Norwich. Not quite.

Take a bow, Norwich

It would be nice to think Norwich began with a bang. But it didn't. Sometime in the eighth century, the various tiny settlements near the Wensum began to grow and grow...

...and Norwich was born. We think.

Archaeologists have two ideas: either it grew up along the sides of the Wensum (their current favourite idea), or four small villages – Conesford, Coslany, Needham and Westwick – grew together until they made a big clump. But no-one really knows – some archaeologist in the future may find the final pieces of the jigsaw.

Anyway, by about the Middle Saxon period (700-850) a settlement had sprung up.

This was more than like-ly in the area between what is now St George's Street/ Colegate and Whitefriars. And some Saxon ditches have been found on the Millennium Library site.

And does the name 'Norwich' itself give a clue? The 'Nor-' bit obviously means 'north' of something and '-wich' means a settle-ment. Was it called that way because it was north of the Wensum?

So we have our new friends the Saxons happily working and living by the Wensum.

It's all very peaceful, isn't it?

Nothing can possibly happen, can it?

Give us a break – this is Nasty Norwich, don't forget. Ladies and gentlemen, sharpen your axes, pick up your shields – or just start running.

The Danes are coming!

The Dreadful Danes

An 'Arrowing time for Edmund

The year 869 was a bad one for the Anglo-Saxon kingdom of East Anglia. But a whole lot worse for its king, Edmund.

He met up with the Danes at Hoxne, on the Norfolk-Suffolk border.

Now, why do you think the Danes had sailed all the way from Denmark, across the North Sea and up the Norfolk coast?

1 They wanted some souvenir tea-towels with 'A Present From Norwich' on it

2 They'd misread their atlas and thought they were going to Norway, not Norwich

3 They wanted to take all the wealth and land they could grab. Oh, and kill a few Saxons too.

Yes, that's right, 3. Edward had guessed correctly too – which is why he tried to defeat the Danes in battle.

But instead he ended up tied to a tree, being used as target practice by their archers. Ouch. Goodbye Edmund.

Goodbye Kingdom of East Anglia...

...Hello Danes.

Land grabbers

East Anglia was in the hands of the Danes for nearly 50 years. It wasn't until 917 that they were finally driven out of the region by Edward the Elder.

Not bad for a man named after a tree*.

What did the Danes get up to while they were here? Well, grabbed all the land they could, for a start. The Anglo-Saxon Chronicle – a book which tells the history of late Saxon England as it happened – says that in 880 the Danes went from Cirencester [that's right over in Gloucestershire] into East Anglia and grabbed and shared out the land. The fast-growing settlement of Norwich would have been a tempting prize.

(* *Not really*)

Disappearing Danes

We don't have much evidence for the Danes in Norwich, although we know they must have been there.

Archaeologists think they could have settled north of the river, in an area that could have looked a bit like Jorvik (Viking York). It certainly would have smelled like it, with lots of mud, animal and human poo and smoky fires.

'I wish someone would hurry up and invent chimneys!'

Someone must have had some money, though. A tiny Viking gold ingot – the first ever found in Britain – was discovered on the Millennium Library site.

A bank and ditch have been found in St George's Street which probably dates from this period. And, er, that's about it.

The trouble, you see, is that there are lots of protected historic buildings in that part of Norwich. No-one would want to pull them down just to answer our Danish questions, even though we're itching to find out.

So we'll just have to wait for the answers for, oh, a few hundred years or so!

Place names give us a hint, though.

Just put down this book a moment and go and have a look at the map of the area around Great Yarmouth. Go on, do it right now.

You're still reading this aren't you? Put it down. Now.

We'll twiddle our thumbs here until you come back.

Tum-te-tum-te-tum, tum-te-tum-te-tum...

Right. You're back? Good. Now you'll have spotted lots of place names ended in -by. That's the Danish word for town and shows there were a lot of their settlements there.

Now look round Norwich - there are place names such as Pockthorpe (-thorpe = farm) or streets ending in -gate (= way or street in Danish NOT gateway). So the Danes were here, after all.

All the time, Norwich was getting more and more important. By 925 it was big enough for the Saxon king Athelstan to set up a mint (coin factory) here. The coins have 'Northwic' stamped on them - the very first written reference to Norwich.

Feeling hot, hot, hot!

Remember our friends the Danes? They were driven out of East Anglia in 917, you'll remember. Would they take the hint? What do *you* think?

Back along the coast and back up the Wensum they sailed on and off over the next few decades. One of the worst visits was in 1004, when the Anglo-Saxon Chronicle records that King Sweyn of Denmark came over with his fleet to cause mayhem.

The Chronicle says he went to Norwich 'and completely ravaged and burned the borough'.

Why? Revenge!

Two years earlier the English king Ethelred had ordered the massacre of lots of Danes in Britain... including Sweyn's sister.

Sweyn must have caused plenty of damage in Norwich, because even hundreds of years later documents were still talking about buildings north of the river being 'in combusto' – Latin for 'in the burnt area'. As the Danes sailed away and the good folk of Norwich crept back to rebuild their singed thatched huts – most people probably lived around the Tombland area by this time – they must have thought things couldn't get any worse.

'Sweyn? More like swine!'

They were wrong.

Here's what happened next:

1013 The whole of East Anglia surrendered to King Sweyn (oh no!)

1013 Sweyn died (hooray – peace at last!)

1014 His son Cnut – Canute – invaded the whole kingdom (uh-oh)

Another chronicler of the time, Otto the Black, tells of Cnut making 'mailcoats red in Norwich'. And no, we're not talking about some rather attractive new uniforms for the local postmen.

Yes, it's yet more blood-letting, folks.

15

Slimy Saxons vs Dastardly Danes

All that fighting must have meant that there must have been something of a love-hate relationship between the two peoples.

Saxon: 'We don't like you Danes!'
Dane: 'Why ever not?'
Saxon: 'Because your mates keep invading us and burning down our homes.'
Dane: 'Ah yes, but we also bring a lot of trade and prosperity so you  can rebuild our town.'
Saxon: '...All ready for you lot to burn down again!'

We know there must have been a lot of Danes living in Norwich in late Anglo-Saxon times because there used to be two churches dedicated to one of their favourite saints – St Olaf – who was martyred in 1030.

Why being an Anglo-Saxon was a pain

Stepping back in time a bit, we now have archaeological finds which shows that being a Norwich resident had meant having a life which was nasty, smelly and full of disease. Two excavations of late Saxon sites – dating to around 1000 or a bit later – showed just how nasty Norwich could be.

A dig on the site of the Anglia Television offices uncovered around 130 skeletons of men, women and children.

Skeletons are really useful things for archaeologists because they show lots of things like age and a wide range of diseases.

And since they were found on a television station site, what better way of telling you about them than in a similar style... so it's over to the Newsroom at Saxon TV...

ABOUT ANGLO (-Saxon)

'Good evening and welcome to Saxon News.

'**BONG!** Survey finds half of the skeletons are children. So don't expect to live long in Norwich...

'**BONG!** One in 16 of you will have a horrible bone condition which leaves you with non-stop pain behind the eyes...

'**BONG!** You'll have to do really hard physical work which will give you lots of painful strained muscles...

'**BONG!** You'll probably suffer from lack of Vitamin D which will leave you with rickets – mis-shapen bones...

'**BONG!** All this will mean you'll probably die before you're 45...

'**BONG!** And will you *PLEASE* stop hitting me over the head with that metal bucket...'

One curious fact before we turn to the nasty discovery at the other site. One of the Anglia dig skeletons was that of an African woman. Was she a descendant of the Roman population of African origin? Or had she been brought over from her homeland as a slave? We will never know...

And now, as promised, the other nasty site! Digging at Fishergate in 1985, archaeologists found evidence of two especially nasty parasites: trichuris (whipworm) which grew several centimetres long and often left you with pain, anaemia (not enough red blood cells) and constantly in need of the loo; and, even nastier, ascaris (maw worm) which had an unfortunate habit of popping out of parts of your body.

But, hey, what a *great* party trick!

We did tell you it was nasty.

Growing Pains

Norwich had grown despite the setbacks because of its great trading position.

By the 1050s it probably had a population of several thousand and as many as 40 churches. That doesn't sound much today but, believe me, it was BIG by Anglo-Saxon standards.

In fact Norwich was so wealthy it was sending the king an annual gift:

1 £20 in cash (worth much much more in today's money)

2 Six jars of honey (how sweet)

3 A bear – and six dogs to fight him (how not sweet)

So we have a prosperous town, which is minting its own money, is a big regional centre and its townsfolk are happy.

Well, happyish.

Still, nothing can possibly go wrong this time.

Er, sorry – ever heard of a guy called William the Conqueror?

The Nasty Normans

Big bully

The first thing William the Conqueror needed to do after giving Harold one in the eye at the Battle of Hastings in 1066 was to show everyone who was the new boss. And the best way to do that was plonk great big castles in the middle of their towns.

Norwich's first castle was probably being built only a few years after 1066. William didn't have time – yet – to build them in stone so the original Norwich Castle was probably an earth and timber affair. Even so, it was HUGE by Saxon standards and the biggest thing yet built in Norwich.

Castle calamity

Here's a quiz. Let's say you're a Norman noble who wants to build a castle in Norwich.

So, do you:

1. Be very nice and put it on some open space west of the Anglo-Saxon town which doesn't bother anyone, except for three field mice and a vole called Kevin.

2. Plonk it on top of 98 Anglo-Saxon houses and two (or even three) churches.

That's right, 2. These ARE nasty Normans, after all. What better way of showing who is boss than by putting hundreds of tons of earth on your nice neat thatched hut. Guess who ended up building it? Yes, the poor old Anglo-Saxons! Perhaps the dastardly Danes weren't so bad, after all.

Norwich, version 3.0

A nice new castle needed a nice new town. So the Normans built one.

And you can still see it – or the streets of it, anyway. Go up to the battlements at Norwich Castle and look toward City Hall. You will see a nice neat grid of streets with Rampant Horse Street on the left, St Peter Mancroft in the middle and the Guildhall and St Giles on the right.

The Normans loved straight lines almost as much as the Romans. If you visit Bury St Edmunds or New Buckenham you can see other examples of their towns.

Every town needs a market, so the Normans moved the Anglo-Saxon market from Tombland to where it is now. And they must have done something right because it's still there 950 years later...

So that makes three goes at making a town: the Danes north of the river, the Anglo-Saxons around Tombland – and now the Normans. And all the time Norwich was getting bigger... and waking up the interest of some very greedy men.

Let's meet one of the nastiest.

Rotten Ralph

A nasty big castle needs a nasty person to run it. Say hello to Ralph de Guader.

Ralph was a big buddy of King William. Not only was he a top Norman, he was also given an earldom, Norwich Castle and the city too in 1071.

Was he satisfied? Oh no. Because our Ralph was a really rotten Ralph. A nasty, scheming ambitious one.

First of all he married noblewoman Emma in 1075, the daughter of loyal William the Conqueror follower William fitz Osbern. At their wedding Ralph got together with Emma's brother and decided it would be a good idea to rebel against the king. Even the reward of being made an earl was not enough for ungrateful Ralph to plot rebellion.

Of course, when the king got to hear all about this he was more than a little cross. So he sent soldiers to besiege the castle while Ralph was abroad raising an army.

That left plucky Emma in charge of the castle. She encouraged the defenders to hold on, but eventually, after three months, the king's army took it. Rotten Ralph's Revolt was Routed.

So what happened to Ralph's supporters? Well, the lucky ones were banished.

So what about the unlucky ones?

Were they:

1.   Given a severe telling-off from William and told they jolly well better not do it again (no).

2.   Fined two weeks' pocket money (no)

3.   Blinded (unfortunately, yes).

As for Ralph, he hopped over in safety to Denmark with his wife.

Perhaps it was all this fighting which led some worried town person to bury a hoard of William I pennies in London Street. He was right to be afraid – he never came back to collect them.

He either forgot where he'd put them – or he suffered an, er, 'accident'. It was left for the archaeologists to discover them nine centuries later.

There must have been lots of similar sorry tales for the poor townsfolk.

Book worms

The Domesday Book was William's survey of every village and town in the country in 1086.

He wanted to make sure he wasn't missing out on squeezing every possible bit of tax out of his poor subjects. Bad news for them – but brilliant for historians in later centuries.

It's because of the mention in the Book that we know of the 98 homes flattened to make room for the castle.

Now here's a funny thing – they didn't mention the churches they destroyed too. That part of the sorry tale was only uncovered in later excavations.

So were Will's scribes a bit reluctant to tell the world what the Normans had *really* been up to?

The Book also shows the impact Rotten Ralph's wrecking and other fire damage had done to the town – there were no fewer than 190 properties standing empty.

Poor Norwich. The nasty Normans had carried on where the devastating Danes had left off.

Castle, Palace – and Jail

The big cheese
Norwich Castle was built by the Normans to get one simple message across: *we're* the bosses now.

William needed to make sure the thriving Anglo-Viking town of Norwich – by now the fourth largest in England – was firmly under his control.

That's why the giant motte (castle mound) was going up within a few months of the 1066 invasion, and the timber castle built as soon as possible.

You might think wood = flimsy, but don't forget that Norwich Castle version 1.0 was tough enough to resist William's troops for three months in the 1075 revolt.

By the 1090s, if the poor English townsfolk needed a reminder where all their taxes were going all they had to do was take a walk down to the Yare, where they could see fleets of barges making their way into the city, full of expensive limestone from Normandy destined for the castle and cathedral.

Going up...
We don't know exactly when work started on the castle, as no building accounts have survived. It was probably around 1094, during the reign of William's son William Rufus. We know it must have been finished by 1121 because Henry I decided to hang his Christmas stocking there.

They must have been in a hurry to start work on a stone castle, because they didn't leave enough time for all the soil in the mound to settle. Result: cracks in the east side.

We shouldn't be surprised a king was coming to visit because the castle, you see, was built as a Royal Palace – the main residence for the king in East Anglia. As well

'This new Castle isn't all it's cracked up to be!'

as the keep, there were a massive 9.3 hectares of earthworks and ramparts – equivalent to more than ten football pitches, and the largest in the country.

The outer bailey ditch used to run right up to St John the Baptist Church on Timberhill, and that's why roads like Market Avenue and Cattlemarket Street run the routes they do today.

This place was MASSIVE! It's impressive now, even with the Norwich skyline full of big buildings and office blocks. But just imagine what the humble folk of Norwich must have felt as they sat in their one-room timber shacks in 1121: very, very tiny.

Which was, of course, just what the Normans wanted.

Revolting times

Whoever controlled the castle controlled Norwich – and whoever controlled Norwich controlled Norfolk and Suffolk, the two most densely-populated counties in England at this time.

That's why it was a key point of the 1075 revolt, and also in 1173 when Hugh Bigod landed in England with a company of Flemish archers. Now Hugh, yet another nasty Norman noble, had been given Norwich by the king and, naturally, HB expected the city to back him in a revolt alongside Henry II's son. But Norwich didn't. So what did Bigod do?

a. Get very cross and throw his favourite teddy from the castle ramparts

b. Send his Flemish boys home with several 'Souvenir of Norwich' teatowels.

c. Capture and burn the city to show how really angry he was.

That's right, C. So poor old Norwich had to burn down – again – so Bigod could show that he was hot (and nasty) stuff.

Norwich's French lesson

The castle's next big problem came not from revolting Normans but some revolting French. King John had proved such a rotten king that the Pope had awarded the Kingdom of England to Prince Louis of France instead.

Louis spent much of 1216 and 1217 ravaging Norfolk and Suffolk including, of course, poor Norwich. All those earthworks and stone walls did no good at all, because Louis took the castle without a struggle in 1217.

After the English finally bid *au revoir* (that's polite French for 'good riddance and never come back') to their unwelcome foreign visitors, they set about making the defences much stronger, with a gatehouse and a ditch ten metres deep to stop others attackers sprinting over the moat bridge.

It didn't help that the good folk of Norwich saw those nice big ditches as very useful rubbish bins.

For almost as soon as the builders had disappeared round the corner, wiping their sweaty brows, the townsfolk were sneaking over and chucking in all the animal bones, broken pots and nastier things they didn't want to clutter up their own homes.

In fact they spent much of the 400 years from the 14th to the 18th centuries throwing their litter into the ditches. Every so often people were prosecuted for dumping, or workers employed to clear them out again – only for the rubbish to start collecting again almost immediately.

Anyway, back to our newly-cut super-duper improved castle defences.

Sorry, did we say 'super-duper'? We meant 'rubbish-wubbish'. Fifty years later rebel barons were able to ransack Norwich, kidnap lots of leading citizens for nice fat ransoms – and carry away, allegedly, 140 cartloads of goodies. And having a castle didn't help one bit.

Cold comfort

Norwich Castle might have looked impressive but must have been, like most stone castles, a cold and draughty place to live. But the Constable who looked after the castle complex for the king did try his best to be comfortable.

He had a private loo (garderobe) and a suite of apartments which included a nice big fireplace, plus washbasin, several bedrooms and painted walls.

Not much of the original Norman interior of the keep has survived – the building has changed use too much over the centuries – but we do have a few clues about how people lived there.

There are the remains of fireplaces, a chapel, a small kitchen – and toilets.

Not a nice comfy loo in a warm bathroom for our Norman friends. Oh no, no, no.

Their bums were made of sterner stuff.

When they went to the loo they had to sit – four at a time – in one of the alcoves. Let's hope the window had some glass in it, otherwise spending a penny would have been a ch-ch-ch-chilly thing to do!

The toilets faced north to the new Norman town, so the soldiers could keep an eye on things (even while they were on the loo) and make sure no-one was, um, kicking up a stink. So they weren't off-duty even when they were off, pooing.

Most of the soldiers and servants probably lived outside in wooden buildings. Not as grand, but much, much warmer.

'Poo! This really is a bum place to live!'

Castle to jail

It won't surprise you to learn that the castle became used less and less as a military stronghold. It passed from royal owner-ship to that of the city in 1345 and by the end of the 14th century it had taken on a new role – the county jail.

It was to stay Norfolk's most feared lock-up – and place of execution – for more than 500 years. Almost up to the 20th century, in fact.

So it was a jail for a lot longer than it was a royal castle.

Norwich Castle might not have been very good at keeping nasty people out – but it was very good at keeping them in!

Behind bars

The first prisoners were probably being held in wooden buildings in the castle bailey as early as the 1160s. As for what went on in the keep, once again we have only a few scraps of evidence.

There's a small room in the castle basement which was possibly used to keep prisoners as they awaited trial.

But the saddest reminders of the prison past can be found in centuries of the inmates' graffiti scratched on the walls.

Often they show religious subjects – Christ on the Cross, for example. A desperate plea for heavenly help?

One stone slab has the following message, dating from the 13th or 14th century scratched into it. 'Bartholomew for the truth, wrongfully, and without reason, am I confined to this prison.'

So a certain junior member of the Simpson family wasn't the first Bart to say 'It wasn't me!'...

Oops, pardon me

Some idea of what conditions for prisoners were like comes from some records for August 1308. Richard Sapling of Heacham was up before the visiting justices accused of being an outlaw.

Their conversation went something like this:

Richard: 'I admit I used to be an outlaw, my lords – but the king gave me a pardon two years ago.'

Justice: 'Hmmm – can you prove it?'

Richard: 'Why yes, I have it here...' *[holds up a soggy piece of parchment]* '....er, only it got a bit wet while I was locked up in the castle and now all the ink's run.'

Justice: 'Hmm – who do you think you're kidding? Still, I suppose we'd better send off for a copy. Oh, and you'll need to go back into jail while we're waiting. It shouldn't take long. Honest.'

But it took *seven years* to do the quick check – and all that time Sapling was stuck in the castle jail. Getting colder and wetter, like his pardon.

And, after all that, the records don't even show if he was declared innocent!

Crime on their doorstep

One of the quirks about the 9.3 hectares of the Castle area was that, because it was a Royal estate until 1345 the normal Norwich laws didn't apply there.

That meant that if, say, a trader had been found to cheat towns-folk by selling them rotten fish he could escape justice by sprinting down from the marketplace and nipping into the bailey. And there was nothing the townsfolk could do.

'Justice round here is as rotten as the fish'!

The problem became so bad that in the period 1122 to 1345 the area round the castle was known as a 'turpus vicus' – Latin for 'evil neighbourhood'.

But the area also provided protection for a vulnerable part of Norwich society – the Jews. The story of how even being under the king's (supposed) protection failed to help them is not only one of the nastiest incidents in Norwich's history, it is also one of the most shameful.

But before we go there, let's hear about Norwich's *other* amazing Norman mega-building.

Cathedral capers

Now see here...

Step forward, Bishop Herbert de Losinga.

Our Herbert was born in southern Normandy. He became a monk at a place called Fécamp, worked his way up to become prior (chief monk) and attracted the attention of William the Conqueror's eldest son, known as William Rufus.

After William II came to the throne in 1087, Herbert was soon brought over to England and made Abbot of Ramsey in the Fens.

But greedy Herbert wanted more – and this is where he made his biggest career mistake. Or his best career move, depending on which historian you listen to.

Abbot Herbert offered the king £1000 (a huge amount in Norman times) for the right to be bishop of Thetford – plus to make his dad Abbot of Winchester.

He'd judged the king correctly (William II = greedy), but most clergymen hated the buying and selling of church jobs. In fact it was a sin, called 'simony'.

Just how upset they felt is recorded in a verse which was doing the rounds at the time:

'Oh grief, the church is let to sordid [= dirty] hire
The son a bishop, abbot is the sire [=father].'

To make up for a sin, you had to do a penance to say sorry. And Herb the Bish's penance, so it's said, was to move the bishopric – his 'see' – to a certain growing town by the Wensum, and build a cathedral there.

Herbert made sure everyone knew how sorry he was. There are even a few scraps of painting in the south nave which show the story. Now was he really sorry – or just pretending, to make himself look good?

We'll never know. But what's definite is that Norwich ended up with a cathedral. And a beautiful one too.

Site fright

Stop me if you've heard this before. The Normans want to build a massive new building in Norwich. Do they:

A Use a nice greenfield site, inconveniencing three more field mice and a vole called Fred?

B Flatten lots more Anglo-Saxon houses (and at least one church too), this time off Tombland?

You won't need us to tell you, but we'd better: it was B.

Getting started

Work began on the massive project in 1096, with Bishop H himself laying the first stone. So soon Norwich had not one, but two huge building projects going on at the same time. We know that some of the stonemasons switched backwards and forwards between the castle and the cathedral, as they have literally left their marks on both.

'When I said drop everything and get back to work I didn't mean on my foot!!'

They mostly used limestone from Caen, in Normandy, and Barnack in Lincolnshire. You can tell the difference because the Barnack stone is greyer – and full of fossils!

One of the amazing survivals from the period is a collection of 57 letters and 14 sermons from Herbert.

In one he tells the monks: 'Alas, the work drags on and in providing materials you show no enthusiasm. Behold, the servants of the king and my own are really in earnest, gather stones to the spot when gathered... you meanwhile are asleep with folded hands... shuffling and failing in your duty.' In other words, GET OFF YOUR FAT LAZY BUMS AND DO SOME WORK!

31

Getting it right...and wrong!

All right, let's praise the builders first. I mean, what a HUGE (and beautiful) building – and all done stone-by-stone by hand or with just the simplest construction equipment. And what's even more clever is that much of it was built with a mathematical formula in mind (1: square root of 2, if you must know. Ask your maths teacher).

However, with so many people helping to build the cathedral there were minor building errors made all over the place, mostly in decoration. Sometimes whole arches were made a bit wide, or too narrow. Even the galleries in the nave are at different levels.

But, hey, we won't tell if you don't.

Finished!...

...by 1145 it was done, built, finished. Hooray!

But work was never really over for our busy medieval masons. The following year they started on Norwich's second-biggest monastery, Carrow Priory. And let's not forget the huge number of medieval churches that they built over the years – supposedly one for every week of the year (and a pub for every day, but that's another story).

Even today Norwich has more medieval churches than London, Bristol and York put together – and more than *any other city* in Western Europe!

...or was it?

In truth, work hasn't stopped on the cathedral for more than 900 years. Bishops were always tinkering with bits and pieces, or adding improvements of their own. And repairing things after disasters. The first disaster hit in 1171 – less than 30 years later.

It wouldn't be the last.

A major fire swept through the cathedral. You can still see where the flames turned the white limestone pink.

Strange habits

We talk of 'Norwich Cathedral' nowadays. But for the first few centuries of its life, the building was the centre of a large monastery complex. Most of its buildings have disappeared, or been converted to other uses over the years. But you can still walk round the cloisters just like the monks did.

There were several types of monks, and most large medieval towns had several varieties. Norwich at one time or another had the Carmelites, Greyfriars as well as others.

Our Cathedral sort were called the Benedictines. You could tell a Benedictine monk by his distinctive habit – or gown – of black cloth.

'Here's that material you were after – just don't make a habit of it!'

There were up to 67 of them at any one time, although a figure nearer 50 is more likely for most of the time. As well as the monks there were all sorts of other people, from cooks and servants to clerks and grooms, taking the monastery's community up to 270 people.

Days for our monks began at 2am in winter – and even earlier in summer.

They spent hours in private prayer and services and only had their main meal 10-12 hours later, depending on the season. After a brief afternoon snooze, it was more work, prayers and – you've guessed it – another service.

Then it was supper and lights out – at 7pm.

And that's not counting the special activities for saints' days and other church anniversaries.

33

Food and stink

They didn't go hungry, our Norwich monks. They ate pork, mutton, beef, chickens, pigeons, fish, vegetables and spices – plus two pounds (0.9kg) of bread a day each.

But the most amazing part of the diet of our 270 people was just how many eggs they scoffed.

Records show they put away up to 13,000 – yes, **THIRTEEN THOUSAND** – every week. That works out about 48 each every seven days. Phew. And poo.

'We have plenty of food but we can't seem to find any friends...'

We better point out that when the cathedral spire was blown down in 1361/2, it was not, um, home-made wind which was to blame...

Money, money, money

As you can probably guess, building and running the cathedral and monastery was not cheap. The Church had grants of land to help bring in cash, but they were always after more money.

Here's four fund-raising ideas which Norwich tried out:

1 **Sweet-talk kings**. William II and Henry I both gave valuable manors to the cathedral in its early years. This meant the bish could drop not-so-subtle hints for other people to follow in their rulers' footsteps and PAY UP!

2 **Offer short-cuts to heaven**. There was a strong medieval belief that giving to the church made up for past naughtiness and helped you get to heaven quicker, or as Herb the Bish once put it 'alms extinguish sin as water does fire'. In other words PAY UP!!

3 **Start a shrine**. This was always a popular choice for religious sites.

Places like Broomholm Priory near Bacton got rich (and famous) by claiming to have a piece of Christ's cross. Other places showed bones of saints. Norwich tried this with its home-grown saint, St William, in the late twelfth century. But after an encouraging start – pilgrims were soon reporting miracles as happening every ten days! – offerings fell to just two pence a year by 1363.

4 **Get a rich local family on your side**. The bishops were not very successful in this, as the rich city fathers preferred to lavish their wealth on other churches. But in the fifteenth

'What about these socks? – They're "holey"...'

century they attracted one of Norfolk's fastest-rising families, who helped pay for improvements to part of the cathedral damaged in a 1463 fire.

But the family soon took its money elsewhere. Which was a shame, because within three generations one of them would be queen of England. Her name? Anne Boleyn.

In the firing line

From early on there seems to have been rivalry between the city authorities and the Cathedral.

The reason isn't hard to see – even today the Cathedral close and buildings are split off from Tombland by two gates and walls. In medieval times this was a world apart, with its own rules and taxes.

The evidence is limited, although we know one row was ended in 1205 when the city and priory agreed that the citizens had pasture rights on church land in Lakenham and Eaton.

But the tensions must have been growing, because in 1272 came one of the most violent incidents in Norwich's nasty history...

1272: The burning of the Cathedral

It all started in June that year in Tombland. There was a fair being held there - and men from the city and priory ended up having big fights. One citizen was even killed by a crossbow bolt, and things soon went from bad to worse.

More fights followed, and when the prior brought in some men from Great Yarmouth it was the signal for riots to start.

'I've always said the townsfolk were revolting – now I KNOW they are!'

Citizens marched on the cathedral on August 11 demanding the prior hand over the Yarmouth men for trial.

But the gates into the close were shut in their faces.

Furious, the townsfolk had archers climb up to the top of St George's Church in Tombland and shoot burning arrows into the cathedral yard.

The cathedral's bell tower and nearby St Ethelbert's Church burned down in the attacks. The cathedral – including the spire and the nave roof – and the cloisters were badly damaged as the mobs rampaged through the priory.

A chronicler wrote: 'They killed many members of the monastery's household in the cloister and within the monastery precincts.

'Others they dragged off and put to death in the city, while others they imprisoned.

'After they had gained entry, they looted all the sacred vessels, books, gold and silver, and everything else that the fire had spared... the citizens continued their burning, killing and plundering for three days.'

The Bishop of Norwich, meanwhile, shut himself up in his palace and prayed for everyone to go away and leave him in peace. The rioting had to end sometime, of course, and when it did someone was going to pay.

They did.

King Henry III himself came down to Norwich to sort out the mess. Thirty of the riots' ringleaders were hanged or burned at the stake, and the city had to pay the cathedral the colossal sum of 3000 marks within six years.

When the city had cleaned up all the mess, a flood hit it the following year which one chronicler from Bury claimed caused even more damage than either Louis' 1217 raid or the 1272 riots.

And the cathedral hadn't seen the end of calamity.

More death and destruction!
In 1361 (or 1362, depending on the historian you ask) a great storm blew down the spire. Never mind, said the priory, we'll build it again. So they did.

And in 1463 it fell down *again* – this time starting a big fire in the presbytery (you can still see the scorch marks).

So it was rebuilt again. This time, the spire stayed up – hooray! It's still there.

Which is pretty good considering it weighs 500 tons and the stones covering the bottom of the 96-metre spire only *lean* on the bricks inside!

The fighting Bishop...
So you thought all bishops were kindly and mild-mannered folk? Not Henry Despenser. This 14th-century bish came to the notice of the Pope through his military activities in Italy – a skill which would come in very handy when revolting peasants made things hot for Norwich in 1381 (see next chapter).

...and the big-headed one
Another bishop who attracted the attention of the Pope was Thomas Brouns, who ran the cathedral from 1436 to 1445.

Brouns the Bish's claim to fame was that he was one of the most pompous holders of the office – ever! He even complained to the Pope about other people wearing posh church clothes when he was around. Every time he visited the cathedral he wanted to be met by a procession at the west door. Oh, and the bells had to be rung too.

You might think that if all the cathedral had to worry about was ringing bells, then its turbulent times were over. But as we'll soon discover, more 'revolting' times lay ahead...

The happy hermit
But just before we go there, let's meet one of the most famous people in Norwich. In fact this person was one of the most famous in the whole country in her day.

And we don't even know her real name!

She was an anchoress, a sort of religious hermit, who lived in a tiny room (called a 'cell') off St Julian's Church (near what is now Rouen Road) around 1400.

She had religious visions, and wrote them down in a book – the first one ever written in English by a woman. She called herself 'Julian', after the saint.

People flocked to ask her advice (a bit like a modern-day agony aunt), while she stayed in her room and prayed alongside a reminder that she wouldn't live forever.

The reminder? Her own freshly-dug grave...

Revolting Norwich

Tense city
Norwich was a bustling, generally thriving place in the Middle Ages. Being a trading centre must have meant people from many nationalities and backgrounds working together. But, as we've already seen, Norwich had its share of rows which sometimes ended up in violence. Here's the story of three more of those times when Norwich was a revolting place to be... literally.

1190: The Jewish persecution
Jewish people were a tiny minority in several important English towns and cities in the early Middle Ages. But many people regarded them with suspicion, superstition – and even fear. The origins of this went back to the Bible, where the Jews were blamed for the death of Jesus. Some people even thought they were friends of the Devil himself.

While all this was going on, the Jewish people living in Norwich – there were perhaps 200 of them at the very most – went about their daily lives.

Most arranged loans, but others were merchants.

They lived in the area between the castle and the Normans' new planned town, around Saddlegate (White Lion Street).

It was no accident – they wanted to be close to the castle for protection.

On March 20 1144 William, the son of a prominent local farmer, vanished. A week later his body was found at Thorpe Wood, 'with his head shaved and punctured with countless stabs'. The boy's mother and a local priest accused the local Jews of murder – and soon Christian servants in a Jewish house started to claim they had seen the boy killed in the same way as Jesus had been.

All crazy nonsense, of course.

But the king's sheriff still had to take the Jews into safety in Norwich Castle until the fuss had died down.

The trouble is, it never did. Soon miracles were being claimed for the site where the body had been found, and the townsfolk started calling the boy 'St William'. One monk from Cambridge even claimed that Jews in Europe had made a secret agreement to kill a Christian child every year around the time of Easter.

Then the Third Crusade (1189-90) saw these 'ritual murder' claims picked up by mobs throughout the country – including London and York.

On February 6 1190 crowds ransacked every Jewish house in Norwich, killing everyone they found there – only those who had fled to the castle escaped.

It didn't end there. Norwich Jews were persecuted again in the 1230s over claims that they had injured a five-year-old boy – and a few years later three were hanged over the incident.

The 'ritual murder' claims – which began right here in Norwich, don't forget – were to be used as an excuse by Christians to massacre Jews across Europe for centuries.

And it won't come as a surprise that *none* of these claims has ever been proved to be true.

1381: The Peasants' Revolt
The pressure for change in Medieval England had been grow-ing for centuries, with ordinary folk yearning for a fairer deal

from their lords and church – both of who took tons of taxes from them. When the Government tried to impose a poll tax on the peasants – forcing them to pay for every single member of their family – it was the final straw. Rebellion started up in Essex, soon spreading to other parts of the country.

The local revolt was led by Geoffrey Lister (or Litester), a dyer from Felmingham.

He gathered his peasant army on Mousehold Heath where they swept into the city. The mob killed nobleman Sir Robert Salle, with Lister beheading a magistrate.

The peasants rampaged through the streets of Norwich, destroying the homes of nobles and lawyers. They ransacked Carrow Priory, burning all the documents they could find. They thought: no documents, no tax.

But the Bishop of Norwich, Henry Despenser, was determined to put a stop to this.

He got an army together and marched on the rebels. Lister and

'OK, you lost – don't get so cut up about it...'

his mob were forced to a last stand near North Walsham, where they were beaten.

Bishop H then sat in judgement on Lister, found him guilty, gave him his last Christian rites – and then walked alongside him to the scaffold. Lister was hung, drawn and quartered for his actions (well, they had to make *absolutely* sure he wouldn't be getting up to any more tricks).

It must have been this revolt which sparked a beefing-up of Norwich city defences a couple of years later. Guns were brought up from London, to be spread over the 40 towers and 12 gates of the wall.

The city fathers were determined that no way would they be caught out next time. But they were!

1443: Gladman's Insurrection

This rioting had a curious start. Local troublemaker John Gladman rode through the city streets on January 22 dressed as a king.

The crowds rioted – not in protest at Gladman's terrible impression of Henry VI (he would never have won Royal Stars in Their Eyes), but against our old friends, the Church. The 3000-strong mob wanted to get into the Priory so they could destroy its tithe documents – the papers which gave the Church the power to tax the citizens. They piled wood against the (firmly closed) gates of the Close, pointed cannon towards the priory and rioted for a week.

And the rioting with the curious beginning had a curious (and happy) ending too: no-one ended up killed by the rioters – and not one of them was hanged. But the mayor was thrown into the Fleet jail in London for six weeks and fined £50.

Just like in 1272, though, the city ended up being fined too. It eventually paid 1000 marks to the cathedral to pay for all the damage.

The city fathers ordered more improvements to the city defences 18 years later because of fears that the national unrest over who should be king (Henry of Lancaster vs Edward of York) would engulf Norwich. All but five city gates were kept locked – the handful that were open had extra guards put on them.

And later that year the Assembly ordered shopkeepers to have ready 'as many staves as they have men servants in their shops, for preserving the peace within the city and for resisting rioters and rebels who desire to disturb the peace within the city'.

Not all the staves in Norwich could save the city from its worst-ever unrest. But for that, we'll have to wait until 1549...

In Sickness and in Health (But Mostly Sickness!)

Kicking up a stink

If you rode into Norwich in the Middle Ages you would have been impressed with the busy-ness of the people and the many churches and the buildings. And then you'd have looked down and realised you had probably trodden in something – and then breathed in and realised that the whole town ponged.

For Norwich, like all other medieval cities, whiffed. It reeked of wood- and turf-smoke (Norwich Cathedral and monastery alone burned 400,000 turves every year), the dung of the many animals kept for trade and in back-yards, stinky occupations, and the pong of human poo.

'It's our latest luxury toilet – the Wensum Poo-Catcher...'

Toilets were primitive, to say the least. When the posh Norman house which now underlies the new court complex was built its owners had the very latest toilet facilities... a shaft going straight down into the river.

That's right, the same river that everyone took their water from. Yuck! And, don't forget, this was at the *posh* end of town.

In 2000 archaeologists found an 11th-century public toilet on land at Fishergate. It was full of layers of straw, scattered over each layer of poo to hide the sight – and smell.

And the diggers found lots of well-preserved poo as well. There, and we bet you thought archaeology wasn't glamorous!

A fine city mess

To be fair, the civic bigwigs in medieval Norwich did *try* to keep the place at least a little bit tidier than the Anglo-Saxons had. The civic records are full of their efforts to get the not-so-good folk of Norwich to be just a teeny bit tidier.

In 1289, for example, William Le Skinner was fined for *(turn away, fans of felines)* throwing bodies of cats into pits and thereby polluting the water supply.

In 1380 the city assembly declared that no-one should carry muck by boats on the river, and people who'd let dung pile up in the streets had to clear them by June 24 – or face massive daily fines of 40d.

And ten years later William Gerard (what is it about Williams?) was fined a pound for leaving *(pony lovers, it's your turn to skip the next bit now)* a dead horse in the road 'to the abominable offence and poisoning of the air'.

Charmed, we're sure.

Unclean! Unclean!

All that dirt and grime led to some nasty diseases. And, before 1348, the most feared was leprosy, an extremely unpleasant skin condition. Recent excavations of 11th-century graves in Timberhill showed a fifth of the people had the disease.

44

In fact, anyone who had any sort of skin condition was in danger of being branded a leper. People were terrified of catching it and so lepers were forced to live outside towns and villages – and that's why we still say 'treat someone like a leper' to this day.

But townsfolk like our old friend Bishop Herbert de Losinga still remembered they had a Christian duty to help the sick. So Bishop H built a special hospital for them between 1101 and 1119. The leper hospital of St Mary Magdalen was built just off what is known today as Sprowston Road.

In Bishop Herbert's day it would have been a little away from the road but close enough to several routes so that the lepers could beg for alms (money) from passers-by. The remains of the building – now known as the Lazar House – have survived until the present day.

And so have the remains of some of its inmates, excavated over the centuries and which show the terrible effect leprosy had on their bones.

Living in the Lazar House
Life wasn't easy for our lepers. Apart from the ordeal of their disease, they:
...had to attend religious services seven times a day to pray for a cure
...needed to beg to survive
...couldn't talk to non-lepers – unless they were down-wind of the healthy people

Even getting food was sometimes a struggle. No-one wanted to get too close to the lepers, and the city fathers even passed a rule in 1473 that the lepers' food buyer wasn't able to touch any of the food he was trying to purchase.

But it wasn't all bad – they had a annual fund-raising bash – the Magdalen Fair.

Not that the lepers were invited, of course. Ever.

Healthy option

Norwich was quite forward-thinking when it came to health care. The Hospital of St Paul (between Mousehold Heath and the river) was built in the early 12th century and had places for 20 poor or frail people – including pregnant women and nursing mums.

Then there was the Great Hospital, built in 1249 and one of the earliest hospitals in the country, with at least 30 beds for sick and poor people.

But death was a fact of life in medieval Norwich, like all cities and towns. There's a famous memorial tablet in Norwich Cathedral which has the picture of a skeleton on it and these cheerful lines: 'All that you do this place pass by/ Remember death for you must dye/As you are now then so was I/And as I am so that you be...'

And the brutal fact was that all the health care in the world couldn't stop the nastiest disease of them all...

...THE BLACK DEATH!!

Plague and Pestilence

A city of dreams....

It's 1349 and everything in Norwich is lovely. Well, OK, so it whiffs but there's tens of thousands of people living here, making it the second-biggest city in the country (and one of the richest).

There's a nice castle, impressive cathedral, four large friaries, several hospitals, almost 60 churches, a thriving waterfront and a busy market.

In fact Norwich is doing so well that its newly-completed walls enclose an area bigger than London and Southwark combined. All right, so most people live in either timber-built or clay-walled houses, in one room mostly, with all their animals and pet parasites.

And there's that pooey rubbish that the civic bigwigs keep trying to get cleaned. Still, nothing that a peg on the nose can't cure.

And then, the Black Death arrives.

Brought from Asia on returning ships, courtesy of black rats and their fleas, it arrived in Weymouth in Dorset on June 25 1348. It spread quickly through the country. The people who rushed to warn other towns took the fleas (and the disease)with them. Norwich's impressive city walls may have been built to stop an army – but they couldn't stop a flea.

It didn't help that Norwich must have been full of rats. There's even a local place name (Muspole) which means the rat-infested pool.

A postcard from Norwich

...that turned into nightmares

No-one knows how many people died when the plague struck. Thousands, certainly – probably tens of thousands. One historian put the figure at 57,304, a ridiculously high amount but even so, the best modern estimate is that the population of the city had plummeted to just 7000 by the 1370s.

Counting the dead was the last thing on anyone's mind. Just surviving was all that mattered. But there are clues – no more than that – in the historical records and through excavation.

They show building works slowing down or stopping completely. For example, the cathedral records show that on June 25 1349, all the building work on the site stopped and everyone went home. Half the monks died, which set people wondering that if God couldn't protect holy people, then what chance did *they* have?

And by 1357 many shops and market stalls had fallen to ruin – no-one to man them, and no-one to buy.

Most scary of all, it's around now that many churchyards were extended to make room for more 'customers'.

'I'm dead certain this is the worst job in Norwich!'

Excavations in 1987 off Magdalen Street in the churchyard of the lost church of St Margaret (used until the 15th century) show many bodies were buried hastily fully-clothed in pits.

There's a really gruesome tale from 1354 which shows

perhaps how bad things were after the plague had swept through.

An assembly order of that year talked about the 'great injuries and dangers' being caused daily by pigs which 'have gone and still go vagrant by day and night without a keeper'.

How dangerous? The order talks of gardens destroyed, houses damaged, people maimed and... children being eaten.

Even dead people weren't safe. They were being dug up by the scavenging wild pigs and... no, that's just *too* nasty to tell.

When packs of wild animals are running unchecked through the streets of a once-bustling city then you know things are very, very wrong.

Killing time

Once the plague was here it kept breaking out every few years, including 1361-2, 1369, 1465, 1471 – when Margaret Paston wrote to her husband about the latest 'pestilence' outbreak and said she was frightened there was 'great death' in Norwich – 1544-5 and 1555-6.

If that wasn't bad enough, there was rampant influenza in the city from about 1550 to 1570.

How many died in all these outbreaks? We don't know for sure until the notorious 1579-80 plague, of which reasonably accurate records survive.

But for that story we'll have to wait until the Turbulent Tudors hit town...

Crime and Punishment (but mostly punishment!)

Law and order

You would think that with a great big castle overlooking the town, people would have thought twice before committing crime. But that didn't seem to stop them, and the law officers were kept busy.

After all, if the townsfolk were prepared to riot they could get up to practically any sort of mischief.

Serious crimes, such as murder, robbery, livestock-pinching and burglary, saw the wrong-doers penned up in the castle until the visiting justices could preside at their trials.

If you were accused of a crime you could pay bail money to the sheriff, which meant you were free until the trial came around (although if it was murder or high treason you were accused of then you just had to stay behind bars).

If you couldn't pay the bail money you stayed in prison any-way.

And waited. And waited.

The justices were supposed to come round every four months. But the slightest hiccup in organising things meant you had to go back behind bars until the problem was sorted out. If we look at the records from 1307 to 1316 they show only one-fifth of suspects being tried in the year of the alleged crime – and a quarter had to wait up to **TEN YEARS** for justice.

You could make your stay in jail more comfortable by paying the jailer for warmer clothes and better food. The jailers got so much money through doing this that they even had a habit of torturing inmates so they would accuse some rich person of a crime. When the rich person was put behind bars, guess who ended asking for lots of cash to make their stay more comfortable...

Chain male (and female)...

As well as the castle jail, you could also be bunged up in the Guildhall from the early 1400s. The complex included a 'clink' underneath, where prisoners were kept in chains. Near the Guildhall was a pillory – a wooden post where your hands were bound while you were whipped. The Cow Tower near the cathedral used to be known as the 'Dungeon Tower' and was another place where you might end up if you got on the wrong side of the law.

An 'offal' diet

You didn't go to prison and come out fat. Food was distinctly dire – unless, of course, you were wealthy enough to pay for the little extras in life, when the jailer would be delighted to oblige (at very reasonable rates, of course). Food was poor quality and just enough to keep you alive.

'Oh goody – mouldy veg again'

If you refused to plead guilty or not guilty you could be ordered to go on an even grimmer bread-and-water diet until you changed your mind. Still, at least the prisoners could look forward to meat.

Well, sort of. In 1421 the City Assembly ruled that any butcher who brought the head of an animal into the market would be made to give it up (plus the lungs and the heart) for the prisoners. Yum, yum.

Wicked warders

Happily, history records one Andrew Asketill, keeper of the cells under the Guildhall, getting his come-uppance in 1534. The city aldermen heard of the many 'grievous complaints' made against him, including selling the prisoners beer at twice the price everyone else paid.

He also took all the prisoners' possessions to pay for the little luxuries of life (like decent food – see above) and if they ran out of cash, kept them in jail until they paid up – even if they'd been found *innocent* of their crimes! Our jailer even drew a dagger and threatened a prisoner.

Nice man. Sadly, the records don't say what happened to him.

Paying the price
There were lots of ways of upsetting the authorities in medieval (and Tudor) Norwich. Here's a selection:

...Being a pain in the bum
If you were a woman who nagged and complained, there was always the risk of being put in the 'cokingstole' – a wooden contraption in which you were forced to sit while being dropped in the Wensum. Joan Mason discovered this to her cost on July 16 1572 when she was taken to the stool, at Jackes Pitt – and drenched. Margaret Grave ('a common scold') was said to have been the last person to have received this punishment when she was given a soaking at the Fye Bridge Street cucking stool in 1587.

Of course, humiliation was the real aim of the punishment.

Just ask John Wyllows.

The Mayor condemned him in January 1549 for his 'evell demeanours' (bad behaviour). His punishment? To be put in the cucking stool with a striped hood – then placed in the stocks (where you were invited to pelt him with whatever bit of rotten vegetables and pongy poo which came to hand). Don't forget this was in the middle of winter...

...Being absent from your master
Apprentices and people legally bound to their masters were punished if they ran away. And servants were *always* running away. Take John Felde, servant to Robart Crispe.

He was sent to prison for three days in 1361 for being absent the same number of days from his master. He'd run away to the country to play music on his 'gitterne' (guitar) instead.

Come on, surely his songs weren't THAT bad?

...Selling strawberries

Yes, that's right. Selling strawberries. As we'll discover in a later chapter, Norwich traders were desperate to keep prices at the right levels to help keep them rich. But they had to be careful not to charge too much money – which is what Thomas Barker and nine others did in June 1562. They dared to sell strawberries at 3d (=1.5p) a pint. For that terrible crime they were threatened with jail...

...Stealing purses

Margaret Bryne was charged with stealing the purse of Mrs Holles' servant in May 1561. She denied the crime, saying her mother and granny had given her the money. But she later admitted handing the purse to her accomplice. Found guilty, Margaret was ordered to be 'whipped with rods'.

She was eight years old.

...Begging

Medieval town officials throughout the country were wary of beggars. They saw them as potential thieves, rioters or religious troublemakers. By the mid-1500s the Government was terrified the number of vagrants was getting out of hand and that social unrest was just round the corner.

Norwich's city walls were not just there to put off would-be invaders – they were there as a way of checking exactly who came in or out.

Beggars who arrived in Norwich were whipped and turned out of the city gates. The civic records note some typical (and not so typical) examples – lots of runaway servants (with guitars, presumably), a one-armed man from Wales and... a bagpiper from Ipswich.

The city must have had a thing about bagpipes, because in 1496 a beggar called Agnes Walkot was ordered to be sent out of the city, with someone walking alongside playing them!

If you came back after being sent away you could expect more severe punishment. Leonard Fox found this out in March 1580.

He had been escorted out of the city five months earlier

accompanied by a jailer who even took him overseas to try to get rid of him.

It didn't work. Len was a glutton for punishment and turned up again in the spring.

This time he was condemned to be tied to a cart and whipped through the streets. And then put in jail for good measure (no mention of bagpipes, though).

History doesn't record what happened then, but let's hope poor Len *finally* got the message.

'...AND STAY OUT!!!'

...Housebreaking

In 1288 Robert Scot was reported as climbing over outer walls at night and gaining entry to houses. Through the door? A window?

No, Robert preferred a more direct entry – through the walls! Housebreaking, literally.

This snippet of information is useful to archaeologists because it shows that house walls were just wattle and daub (sticks with clay spread on them). So Burglar Bob was some use to history – even if he wasn't much use to his neighbours.

...Being rude about the ruler

William White found this out rather painfully on July 12 1550. The Norwich Assembly Book records that he was 'sette upon the pillory and both his ears nailed to the same, and then cut off, for speaking of seditious wordes'. Compulsory ear-piercing also happened to Robert Gold in 1554 for publishing 'unfitting songs against the Queen's Majestie'. Ouch.

'This 'ere punishment is cruel!'

...Setting fire to things

Arson was actually quite a rare crime – most criminals wanted to pinch property, not burn it. In 1264 William de Eblaster and others burned down the house of John de Ballaga by setting fire to its gate. How do you think they made sure they were successful? Did they:

A. Put holes in the fire buckets,

B. Remove the clappers and ropes of bells from nearby churches so the alarm could not be raised, or

C. Block the river to stop water being gathered?

The answer's B – let's just hope John 'tolled' someone about the fire somehow.

...Murdering someone

As you can imagine, this was always frowned upon (unless you were a Jew in the 12th century, apparently).

One strange case came in 1415 when William Koc of Trowse was murdered in Lakenham by a gang armed with spades and sticks.

When attempts were made to arrest the culprits, the Priory at Carrow said: 'No you can't! That bit of land belongs to us, so our church rules apply – not yours!'

As you might expect, this did not go down too well with the city fathers, who hit on a way out of the problem: accuse prioress Edith and another nun of the murder instead!

So there you have it: justice. Easy when you know how.

...Being a heretic

One of the most dangerous things you could do for hundreds of years was to dispute the official version of Christianity. Such behaviour – known as 'being a heretic' - was seen as striking at the very heart of the Church and of the country itself.

There was only one punishment and, boy, was it nasty.

Among the city records for 1427 is a routine list for expenses. These include items such as the repair of signs, buying bread for the mayor's table and the like.

Oh, and these two: 'two cartloads of wood bought in the market for burning William Qwyette, heretic' and 18d (7.5p) spent on 50 faggots (bundles of twigs) to burn William Waddon and Hugh Pye.

A religious group known as the Lollards was persecuted from 1401 and a slope of land just outside Bishop's Bridge was known as the 'Lollard Pit' because of the many martyrdoms which took place there.

But as we'll see in a later chapter, things got worse later in Tudor times. Much, *much* worse.

Getting away with it

It's not all gloom. There were several ways you could try to evade justice.

And we have to say some were *rather* better than others. So let's see if you can guess how these ideas turned out...

1 **Claim it was self-defence.** As on October 2 1309 when justices at Norwich Castle heard from John le Walsche, accused of murdering Richard Cous after a row.

He said that Richard had drawn a knife and chased him into a corner, where John drew his sword – and Richard obligingly ran into it. But was he found guilty?

2 **Be pregnant.** You can't say the medieval authorities weren't caring. If you were found guilty of a crime and found to be carrying a baby, like burglar Agnes Vincent in 1316, then they didn't punish you... or did they?

3 **Say you were tortured.** As we've seen, the jailers were not amiss to a bit of pain-giving if it meant they could make more money. John Bonde told the court in 1310 that he had been forced to make false accusations.

The court report went on: 'He testifies that the constable of the castle forced him to make the appeal through various tortures, beatings and starvation which were carried out in the lowest room of the gaol'.

The constable, no doubt, was giving his best "surely not poor little old innocent me" looks while all these claims were being made. So who did the court believe?

'...and after I lock them up I tell them all a bedtime story... honest'!'

4 **Tell fibs.** Of course, all the criminals tried this one. But we especially like the efforts of convicted thief John Kynnon, who put off his execution by naming three accomplices who'd helped him. Officials then spent *two years* trying to track down 'Jonathan of Cottenham', 'John Bindedenell' and 'William of Tostock' before jurors decided in 1314 he was telling a pack of lies.

So what happened next?

5 **Plead insanity.** It might surprise you that medieval juries were very sympathetic in cases of what we would now call mental illness. Andrew Friday was accused of stealing a horse and trying to sell it in Norwich market in June 1307. He was guilty – but evidence was given how he had chopped down all the trees at his home and then tried to replant them, and how he went insane every time the moon was a certain size. What did the court decide to do?

6 **Fight a duel.** You had the right to challenge your accuser to a fight to prove your innocence. Geoffrey atte Bush tried this one in October 1309 after being accused of murder by Richard Quynchard. But cunning Richard said he couldn't fight because he was missing two fingers on his right hand. So who won the case?

7 **Claim 'benefit of clergy'.** The Church had its own laws. If you could prove you were a church official, you couldn't be convicted by an ordinary court. It didn't matter if you were accused of robbery or even murder. You had to give up your property to the king, and there was a sort of trial in front of the bishop – but it was still a great way to get away with nasty crimes. Cheating justice in this way did not go down well with the victims' families. So how many got away with this defence between 1307 and 1316?

Was it one in 100, one in 20, or one in ten?

8 Survive hanging. Walter Eghe did in 1286. Found guilty of stealing cloth, he was hanged and taken to the church of St George Tombland. As you can imagine, 'surprised' must have been an understatement of everyone present when 'dead' Walter suddenly revived. So what happened next?

'I see old Walter's hanging around again...'

So let's see how you got on: 1 The jury believed John; 2 The court waited until the baby was born, *then* they hanged Agnes; 3 They believed the constable – Bonde was hanged; 4 He was executed (Nice try anyway, John); 5 He was pardoned; 6 Geoffrey was found innocent – so the court hanged Richard instead for telling fibs; 7 One in ten; 8 He stayed inside the church for 15 days before escaping and eventually getting a king's pardon.

The nastiness of Norwich justice isn't just in the history books. The archaeologists have found evidence of it too. In 1987 the churchyard of the now lost church of St Margaret off Magdalen Street was excavated.

St Margaret was also known as 'St Margaret ubi sepeliunter suspensi' which is Latin for 'where those who have been hanged are buried'. The gallows were only a couple of hundred metres away just outside the Magdalen Street gate.

Among the many skeletons found were ones buried face-down and thrown into pits – and some with their hands tied behind their backs. For these criminals, there was only one brand of justice – the nasty sort.

Terrible Trades and 'Orrible Occupations

Getting down to busy-ness

Medieval Norwich was a busy place. Picture a town packed with people going to and from market, calling in at an alehouse for a quick drink, calling out their wares to try to attract passing trade, having another quick drink (because shouting is thirsty work), going down to the wharves by the river to help load and unload goods – and having another quick drink because that's hot work too...

Amazingly there were more than 130 trades and occupations recorded in Norwich by the 13th century. Perhaps the most important was leather-making – products were made into jerkins (jackets), belts, gloves, harnesses, parchment and much more.

Let's see if you can guess what these people did – these examples are all taken from the late 1200s.

We'll give you six trades: 1 Exsmith, 2 Bukmongere, 3 Dubbatur, 4 Luminur, 5 Panter-maker, 6 Skirmischur.

Now pick from these possible explanations:

a. a person who trims the toenails of pigs;

b. a giraffe impersonator;

c. a maker of axes;

d. a fish juggler;

e. a dealer in venison (deer meat);

f. a wattle-and-daub polisher;

g. a renovator of old clothes;

h. an illuminator of old manuscripts;

i. A worm-tamer;

j. a maker of bird-snares and k. a fencing-master.

Baffled? Then look below..

The answers are: 1C; 2E, 3G; 4 H; 5J; and 6K.

Kicking up a stink...

Noisy and smelly trades were kept on the edge of the city wherever possible, often alongside the river. These nasty activities included leatherworking (which involved animal skins and used poo as one of the ingredients) and fulling (cloth preparation, which used huge quantities of stale wee). Just think what *that* all smelled like!

And the best bit was these industries were concentrated upstream of the city.

So all the nasty smelly waste was washed down towards the houses... just where people drew their drinking water.

'Lovely fresh meat! Lovely fresh meat...'

It wasn't just the Wensum either. Norwich was full of other streams and rivers (now covered up) like the Great Cockey, which ran roughly where Gentlemen's Walk and London Street are now. It stank.

Butchers were another trade which produced some truly 'offal' smells and nasty waste (just imagine the smell in a heatwave, with no fridges).

They were concentrated along Ber Street by the beginning of the 14th century – presumably because the only person who wanted to live next door to a butcher was another butcher. Its reputation lasted for centuries – even in Victorian times it was still known as 'Blood and Guts Street'.

Still, at least the meat they produced must have tasted better than the beef which John Trukhe was caught selling in Norwich market in 1296.

That was taken from a drowned cow he'd happened to find in the Wensum.

61

History doesn't record how long the poor creature had been in the river, but seeing as Trukhe was being prosecuted for it, we can only guess it must have been a long, *long* time.

...and a racket

Blacksmiths were gathered on the edge of the built-up area north of the river by about 1300. This was for two reasons: fire risk (from their coal-burning forges) and noise. Just how irritating it must have been is summed up in this poem scribbled on a Norwich Cathedral manuscript dating from about 1350.

'All right, so my old socks stink – but at least they make good earplugs...'

> *Swart Smoky Smiths Smirched with Smoke*
> *Drive me to death with the din of their dints*
> *Such noise at nights heard no man never*
> *Such crooked codgers cry after 'coal, coal!'*
> *And blow their bellows till their brains are all bursting.*

We don't know who the writer was, but we'll take a guess he wasn't president of the Blacksmiths' Appreciation Society!

Trading places

As well as all the city written records, there is place name evidence too.

Groups of traders tended to stick together (sometimes they still do today – look at all the estate agents around Tombland, for instance).

From this sort of evidence we know, for example, where potters, leather-dressers and dyed cloth producers tended to gather.

Cloth was to become the biggest source of Norwich's wealth for centuries. Some of the many other trades recorded include bell-founders, goldsmiths, parchment dealers, surgeons, glaziers and many, many more.

The rise of the gilds
Traders were keen to form groups called gilds, which controlled the way most trades were run. The King (Edward I) didn't approve, because he was worried the gilds would control trade and use their power to push up prices (which was, of course, exactly what they wanted to do).

In Norwich the tanners got together in 1288 and 1291, and were fined for doing so.

The same thing happened to fullers, saddlers and cobblers in 1293.

But gilds were inevitable. And when they formed, wealth followed.

The city authorities were keen on them because it was easier to impose control of the traders. For example, they could (and did) order them to raise fees to put off outside applicants.

Keep the money in...
Building town walls was a good way of boasting to other places what an important place you were – and were handy in times of trouble.

But perhaps just as important was their role in keeping control of exactly who went in and out of a city.

This was a good way of making sure you kept out the shifty-looking people who might cause trouble – or the travelling merchants who might take away some of the trade from your own shops (but not, apparently, people walking in with drowned cows over their shoulders).

So when Norwich was enclosed with a bank and ditch in 1253, it made a useful trade barrier as well as a defensive one.

63

Food....

Cut the supply of food – or make it too expensive – and you end up with riots. That's why the city fathers kept a close control of who sold what – and for how much. Their strict rules included:

No food to be bought before the bell rung for Lady Mass at the Cathedral, traders to be gathered in one place to ensure competition, and all weights and measures to be checked at least twice a year to stop cheating.

People coming in from the county to sell things in the city had to pay a toll.

But traders tried all sorts of dodges...

In 1290 John de Fransham was caught buying corn outside the city and sneaking it inside at night to avoid the tolls.

And in 1375 a man was caught bringing in cheap oysters from his secret stash at Thorpe.

...and drink

Brewing was very important from the earliest times. For a start the water was often so dodgy that beer was the safest thing to drink.

Even children had it, although their tipple was a weaker version called 'small beer' – which is where we get the expression for something not very important.

Typically, the city authorities tried to strictly control brewing, but were widely ignored. In 1498 you could expect to pay 7d (about 4p) for a firkin (about 45 litres) of best beer and 5d for small beer.

The city assembly did take some action though. In 1471 there were complaints about 'weak and unwholesome brewing'. So they elected two people in each ward (city district) to be tasters. Cheers!

Fur fashion's sake

If you were a fluffy creature in medieval England you were

likely to be patted on the head... then clubbed to death.

Animal skins, you see, were a sought-after commodity for clothes.

Which is why a list of tolls for unloading cargoes along Norwich waterfront in the Middle Ages included charges for skins of beavers, cats, 'grey work' (probably badgers) and squirrels.

As these were charges for cartloads of skins, we can only imagine how many poor battered beavers, bashed badgers, crunched cats and splattered squirrels that all added up to.

Fishy tales

Fish was big news in Norwich. The city had been at the head of the Yare estuary in very early days, which may explain why it still paid an annual tribute of 24 herring pies to the king every year.

A record from around 1350 of what ought to go into the pies has been preserved, so if you can persuade your mum and dad to let you into the kitchen, you could try this recipe.

120 (yes, 120!) fresh herrings
225g ginger
225g pepper
125g cinnamon
27g cloves
27g long pepper
14g grains of Paradise (guinea grains – a sort of spice)
14g galingale (a spice like ginger)

Mix these up and divide into 24.

Add five herrings for each pie. Bake.

The records show Hugh de Curson was charged with the job of taking the pies to the king.

Since the journey to London could take up to ten days, we hope he was equipped with a clothes peg for his nose – and the king had no sense of smell!

Fish was really important in medieval times because it was one of the few things people were allowed to eat in the Lent period before Easter. And the Church said people should eat fish on Fridays, too. It was so important that during the city's Shrove Tuesday procession to mark the start of Lent, there was a man dressed in stinky white and red herring skins.

Bet he struggled to find friends.

Can you dig it

One of the most unusual occupations in medieval Norwich was chalk mining. There was no source of stone within 50 or so miles, so there was a huge demand for flint – and when the city walls starting going up the demand became even bigger.

From late Anglo-Saxon times people had realised that if they dug down through the chalk they could find free flints for building.

You could also use the chalk for extracting lime – another useful building material.

So they dug. And dug. And dug.

The thing is no-one really knows just how much they did dig (or how far). But they were at it, on and off, for almost 650 years.

That's a lot of flint – and a lot of tunnels.

Sometimes these have caused problems in later ages. In 1823 chalk vaults up to two metres wide were discovered near St Giles' Gate, prompting fears three generations later that they would affect the foundations of the Roman Catholic Cathedral.

And in 1936, for instance, a chalk tunnel collapse destroyed a house in Merton Road, killing two people.

And who can ever forget that famous day in 1988 when a bus started to slide backwards down a hole in Earlham Road?

Building up trade

All this building showed Norwich was getting very rich. And if you want a simple illustration of just how, then try this: the building of the city walls.

We've said that huge amounts of flint were needed for the city walls. Just how much can be seen from the fact that they ran in two sections from Carrow to New Mills, and from St Martin-at-Oak to Barrack Street – a distance of more than 3.6 kilometres – the largest area enclosed by any walled town in England during the Middle Ages.

The walls were six metres high, and also included 40 towers and 12 gates. The work also included – and we're back to look-ing after local trade again – two 'great chains of Spanish iron' stretched across the river to regulate traffic.

Amazingly, all of this was largely paid for by one man – Richard Spynk. A grateful city declared on December 10 1343 that Spynk and his male and female descendants were freed of all 'tallages, tasks, and costs, and labours' to do with Norwich for ever.

So if your name's Spink, your mum or dad might like to try that one on the city council the next time they get their council tax bill. But don't tell anyone we told you!

Trade = power

Towns and cities were *always* trying to find ways of getting richer than their rivals. So protecting trade became the number one thing in their minds for centuries (when they weren't rebelling or burning heretics, that is).

Norwich, like other places, was always trying to sweet-talk the king of the day into giving the city 'charters' – written permissions to run their own affairs and have markets and fairs.

Norwich had its first charter around 1158 (thank you Henry II), another in 1194 (the one which historians say is when Norwich became a city - thank *you* Richard I) and in 1404 which gave Norwich the right to elect its own mayor, collect its own taxes and sort out its own justice (big, *big* kisses to you, Henry IV).

Within three years, the newly-independent city was building its handsome Guildhall, considered to be the largest building of its kind outside London.

Paying the price
But just sometimes there was a reminder of the price to be paid for trade – and not just if you were a beaver, cat, badger or squirrel.

In October 1343 a boat packed with onions, wood, coal, herrings, salt and iron was travelling up from Yarmouth to Norwich when it capsized at Cantley. It had been overloaded, you see.

All the goods were lost – and so were the lives of the 40 people on board.

The turbulent Tudors

Troubles ahead...

If you thought the medieval period in Norwich was full of woe, calamity and death, then the Tudors (1485-1603) brought tons more trouble.

The first of them, Henry VII, visited in Christmas 1485.

That cost the city fathers £140 in gifts for their new lord, not counting the stocking-fillers for his nobles. But the true cost of the Tudors was to be much more.

How about fires, riots, the biggest civil unrest in Norfolk's history, plague, more riots, an earthquake and people burned at the stake...

Hot stuff

Let's start with fires. There had been something of a housing boom in Norwich from about 1475.

'I told you to light the barbecue OUTside!'

Most houses were two storeys, timber-framed and covered with thatch.

Which was fine, until there was a big fire, as there was in 1467 – and again in 1507 (twice).

The 1507 blazes destroyed more than 700 houses (that's about four in ten of every home in the city), and archaeologists have found a big chunk of Pottergate which fell victim to the flames.

Top Tudor poet John Skelton wrote a verse about how terrible it all was, describing the fire damage as a 'sad calamity' and how it was goodbye to poor Norwich.

69

'Strong stuff, and after a second fire hit the city two years later, the city authorities ordered all new housing to be built with tile and not thatch to try and stop a repeat performance.

It didn't. As late as 1570 the city authorities were complaining that 'diverse [=lots of] casualties and mischances' kept happening because there were too many thatched houses – and not enough buckets and ladders to fight the fires with.

And even now there are still six houses in Norwich with thatched roofs. Bet you can't find them all!

Weaving a fortune

The old medieval industry of leather-working had been overtaken by weaving – trade which was to dominate Norwich for centuries and keep it as England's second most important city until the 1700s.

Instead of the big gloomy factories which were to come in the Industrial Revolution, the work was done in small gloomy attics in houses across the city. While the men weaved, the rest of the family were kept busy spinning as much wool as they could. If you didn't work, you were in trouble, as we'll see in a later chapter.

Everyone wanted their share of the booming industry – which sparked (you've guessed it) yet more riots. Weavers rioted in 1511 against women who they said were pinching their work – and city fathers also passed laws banning the employment of Scots, Frenchmen or other foreigners.

But you couldn't stop people trying to get their share. It got so bad that in 1560 the city assembly ordered all weaving to stop for a month in August – because the farmworkers were leaving the harvests to head for the city to work there instead.

Hello, Stranger

Norwich has been home to plenty of people from other countries all through its history.

We've already seen the Danes (trading and burning the place down), the Normans (taxing and building) and the Jews (trading and being persecuted).

Now let's say hello to the Strangers.

That's the name city folk gave to the Flemings, Walloons and Dutch who fled from religious persecution in the Spanish Netherlands (now modern Holland and Belgium).

In 1565, the city authorities gave permission for 30 Dutch refugee families to settle in Norwich. Within three years there were almost 1500 Strangers (and this in a city of about 10,000).

The workers brought new skills in weaving, silver-working, pottery, and even gardening. They also set up the first local printing press in 1570. All welcome, you might think.

But local weavers – who'd already moaned about women, Scots and Frenchmen, you'll remember – were in no mood to welcome more rivals.

In 1570 John Throgmorton and other Norfolk gentry tried to start a rebellion to have them expelled. But the uprising collapsed – leaving its ringleaders to be hung, drawn and quartered.

Nothing, not even a near-revolt, could stop the Strangers flocking to Norwich. By 1579 there were around 6000 – that's more than a third of the city's population.

Fitting them all into the city took some doing. The solution was to create a maze of yards and courts behind Norwich's ancient streets. These new houses were crowded, dark, dingy – and smelly.

But full of birdsong. For another thing the Strangers were said to have brought to the city were... canaries.

Royal visit

In June 1578, the city fathers at Norwich were told to expect a very special visitor later that summer: Queen Elizabeth.

The Queen had begun the idea of regional tours – 'progresses' – as a way of meeting her subjects and, hopefully, impressing them with what a great ruler she was.

It was a great honour to have the Queen as a guest. The trouble was, she didn't come on her own.

She needed her courtiers, her ladies-in-waiting. Her clothes. Her bodyguard. Her ministers – and their bodyguards and servants. And so on and so on...

In fact by the time she reached Norwich she probably had about 200-300 people with her. And guess who had to feed them all? That's right, the good folk of Norwich.

But before she arrived, the Mayor ordered a massive clean-up of the city.

Norwich, you'll remember, was a trifle pongy at times. So the orders went out: No dirty streets. All riverside toilets to be scraped clean. No milking of cows in the street. No leaving bits of animals around. No keeping pigs in the Castle Ditch.

Oh, and, definitely, definitely, **DEFINITELY**, no peeing or poo-ing in the streets!

On August 16 a huge civic procession, led by Mayor Robert Wood, rode out to meet the Queen at Harford Bridge. After delivering a speech – in Latin, the great big show-off – he gave her a silver and gold cup with £100 in it.

Good Queen Bess told him: 'Princes have no need of money, God hath endowed us abundantly.' (Not that she gave it back!)

The Queen had an enjoyable six-day stay – despite thunderstorms and rain stopping some elaborate shows which had been planned for her.

In gratitude, she knighted the mayor on her way out of the city. So that £100 had come in useful after all... for someone, anyway!

An 'old friend' returns

It was a few months after the Royal visit that the biggest disaster in Tudor times hit the city. Worse than the religious upheavals, worse than the rebellions.

This was the return visit of an old 'friend' which had been haunting the city for more than two centuries... the plague.

In fact many people said the massive royal entourage had brought the pestilence with them – a claim which historians have doubted.

'This is one souvenir of Norwich I could do without!'

But what is sure is that this was the first plague outbreak for which we have reasonably accurate records.

And what a terrible story they tell.

During the 1579-80 outbreak there were more than 4800 deaths of which almost 4200 were blamed on the plague. That meant for every eight people who died, perhaps seven were killed by the disease.

The population dropped from perhaps 14,000-15,000 to 9000 or so.

In fact some historians believe the Tudor tragedy might even have been as bad as the 1349 calamity.

In August alone 352 people were dropping dead of the plague every single week.

What could the city fathers do?

Not a lot.

They passed laws in 1580 that no-one was allowed out of an infected house unless he was carrying a two-feet white wand – so people could take avoiding action.

And parish sextons were ordered to nail up the doors and windows of badly-affected homes – and stick notices on them saying 'The Lord have mercy upon us'.

They tried this again in 1584-5 and 1589-92 when plague came back, killing at least another 3500.

But when it came to the crunch all anyone could really do was pray.

To little effect. Once again, people were dying to live in Norwich... literally.

Shaken, not stirred

So far in the city story we've had fire, floods, storms and plague. Surely there's no more natural disasters left?

Wrong. How about an earthquake or two?

On December 28 1480 the good citizens suddenly realised the rumbles they could feel weren't the after-effects of the Christmas pudding.

That quake was strong enough to damage the city walls.

Funnily enough, 100 years later, on April 5 1580, history repeated itself. Here's what a chronicler had to say: 'Somewhat before VI of the night [=6pm] there was an earthquake which did so shake the Guildhall that Mr Mayor, the Sword-bearer and the Town Clerk were afraid to tarry [stay] there because the roof of the chamber, being very strongly built with timber, trembled and cracked so sore that they feared the fall of it...'

Spain's a pain

That wasn't the only time the citizens of Norwich were shaking in the 1580s. Only this time they were quaking with fear.

In 1588 a huge Spanish fleet appeared off in the English Channel, with the aim of conquering the upstart little Protestant country of England. Panic swept through the land, and in Norwich people suddenly realised that the city was only a day's ride from the coast.

So they sent 300 men to Yarmouth to reinforce the garrison there. Happily a combination of the English fleet and bad weather meant the Spanish Armada ended in chaos.

You would have thought the horse-rider who rode like mad from Lynn to Norwich to give the good news to the city would have been showered with oodles of cash and the hand of the Mayor's daughter in marriage.

But all he got was five shillings (25p) – just enough to buy a barrel or two of beer.

'Actually, er, I think I WILL just have the beer money...'

But the Armada story didn't end there. Garsett House, at the corner of Prince's Street and St Andrew's Street was said to have been built out of timbers from wrecked Spanish ships in 1589.

And in the same year ace sailor Sir Francis Drake sailed to Portugal and Spain, with several of Norwich's celebrated city musicians (the Waits) on board by his special request. It was a great honour – but one the Waits could have done without. Three of them died on the voyage.

75

The Nine Days' Wonder

Ever heard that phrase? It means something which suddenly and briefly becomes the talk of the town.

And it all began in Norwich. Dancer and actor Will Kemp – a friend of Shakespeare – made a bet that he could dance his way from London to Norwich in nine days.

Will Kemp...

...will need plasters!

On the way he had to contend with pot-holes in the roads and snow. As he danced his way to the finishing post, through cheering crowds, he nearly came a last-minute cropper – by tripping over the petticoats of one of the welcoming committee.

He was so delighted at finishing that he jumped over the brick wall by St John Maddermarket to celebrate. We're amazed he even had the energy!

PS Talking of Shakespeare, it was a Norwich-born writer, critic and hard-drinker Robert Greene who described him as 'an upstart crow'. Why was he so annoyed? He reckoned the Bard had pinched the idea for one of his plays (A Winter's Tale) from one of Greene's own books.

Fair comment... or just sour grapes?

Law and disorder

We've already met some of the villains of medieval Norwich – and how they were punished. So let's meet their Tudor counterparts.

By now the city had another place for punishment – the Bridewell – suitable for minor offenders. You could end up there, say, if you punched someone.

It was either that or be whipped.

Michery was the Norwich word for petty theft – like pinching apples from next-door's orchards. For that you ended up in the stocks if you were a grown-up – or whipped if you were a child.

'Immorality' was a very popular offence, especially in Elizabethan times. If you were caught kissing someone you shouldn't, what do you think happened?

Were you:

A Made to build a model of the Castle out of matchsticks, blindfold, while someone poured jelly over your head?

B Paraded round the city with a paper hat, followed by a crowd banging basins to make sure everyone turned round to look at you?

C Forced to wear the same socks for six months?

If you remember back to medieval times they were big on public humiliation.

So that's right, B (although we bet everyone probably did C anyway. Phew.).

Playing games on a Sunday would cost you 3s 4d (about 17p) – but the law had little effect. And being drunk would cost you five shillings (25p), or six hours in the stocks while everyone laughed and threw rotten tomatoes (or worse) at you.

And talking of being drunk, one notorious Tudor pub was the Three Cranes Inn. One 1567 report described it as 'a tippling house without all order of law, whereto all evil and naughty persons... do retreat'.

And where was this awful, evil pub? In Cathedral Close! Which brings us rather neatly to the subject of Tudor religion. Brace yourself folks – this is where it gets even nastier...

Nasty Religion

Dissent and death

When it comes to religion, the 16th century was the most turbulent in English history. If you disagreed with the official religion, the result could be painful. And fatal.

What made it harder was that the goalposts kept moving.

At the start of the century England, like just about everywhere else, was a Roman Catholic country with the Pope at the head of the Church. And Henry VIII was a keen Catholic like everyone else.

Why, he even went on a pilgrimage to Walsingham when he was young.

If you preached against being a Catholic, you died.

Thomas Bilney, one of the group known as Lollards, was burned at Norwich in 1531. There were about six Lollards burned in the city in the early years of the century.

But when the Pope didn't like the idea of Henry marrying Anne Boleyn, Henry split with Rome and set up his own Church in 1531.

You disagreed? You died.

Then in 1536 he decided to pinch all the monasteries' lands. You disagreed? You died.

Norwich Cathedral and Priory was luckier than most. Power was transferred to a 'Dean and Chapter' in 1538, and the buildings survived relatively undamaged.

But Carrow Priory – Norwich's second largest – was dissolved. All the small friaries in the city were sold off as well.

Among the victims was the College of St Mary in the Fields, founded in 1250 as a hospital but which then became a college for priests. It got splattered in Henry's reforms and ended up as a practice ground for archers in Queen Elizabeth's reign. And that's how Chapelfield got its name....

It was goodbye to the monks of Norwich. Except for one lot...

The great escape
One friary in Norwich managed to escape being knocked down. But only just.

Blackfriars Hall only survives to this day because the city corporation bought it as a meeting place. Funnily enough, it escaped Henry's first grab of monastery lands – because it *had* no land.

But by October 1538 the friars were so poor they begged the Duke of Norfolk to take it over. The place was falling to pieces, with windows broken. They had even had to sell their bell to try to keep the place going.

The top friar was probably given a pension to tide him over, with the monks given a pound each and some ordinary clothes to wear. The friary also had an 'anchoress' – a religious hermit – who was told she could stay 'so long as she shall kepe her shoppe'.

In other words, kept her trap shut!

The city paid £81 for the buildings in June 1540, when it became known as 'New Hall'.

It was soon being used for grand civic parties – the only friary building in England to survive Henry's land-pinching.

At one in 1561, so it's said, the city fathers had the chance to see a pair of the newly-discovered wonders of South America – guinea pigs. And what did they do with these fascinating creatures?

You've guessed it: they ate them.

'Um...er... guinea pig, anyone?"

(The city must have had a thing about persecuting cute creatures. In 1545 the Assembly ordered fishermen to get their dogs to kill the fish-pinching local otters. The rotters.)

Sometime later in that century Blackfriars became linked with the Strangers – and, amazingly, as late as the 1890s there was still an annual service held there in Dutch.

Goodbye Henry, hello Edward

So at least there was one happy(ish) ending for one city friary in all the religious turmoil. But there were plenty more cruel times ahead.

On June 27 1546, shoemaker Edward Bretten was sent for trial in Norwich. His terrible religious crime? Reading the Bible in English.

See what we mean about disagreeing with the official religion?

A year later, old King Henry died, to be replaced by his young and sickly son Edward VI. Powerful nobles took charge and grabbed more land – including some belonging to the Dean and Chapter.

Officials went through churches in Norwich and elsewhere, splatting statues and smashing stained glass because they were linked to the old religion.

How many precious and beautiful things were destroyed? We can only guess.

And about this time (1547), the city took over the old Great Hospital, another religious site. Forty 'poor persons' were to be looked after there, but by 1550 Sir John Fisher was complaining that the men were so lazy that they even left the women to carry bodies for burial. The guys were also fighting, getting drunk and trading punches at meal times. The solution? Take away their meat and put them in the stocks...

Back to the future

After Edward VI died in 1554, his sister Mary came to the

throne. She hated the new Protestant religion, and went back to Catholic ways.

You disagreed? You died.

According to some historians, from 1557-8 Norwich had more heresy burnings than anywhere except London and Canterbury. Almost 50 people met a grisly end at Lollards' Pit, near Bishopbridge (although only two were from the city itself).

Even after Bloody Mary died in 1558, and her Protestant sister Elizabeth became queen, there were still religious rows – even between Protestants.

As late as 1578, wheel-maker Matthew Hamont was burned at the Castle Ditch for saying the New Testament was a 'mere fable'. It was a bad time for him: a week earlier he'd had his ears cut off for telling fibs about the queen. Ouch.

'Look on the bright side – at least you'll save money on earrings...'

And four years earlier, the queen had asked her (Norwich-born) Archbishop of Canterbury, Matthew Parker, to get rid of as many Puritan (extreme Protestant) churchmen as he could.

He failed. And the Puritans were set to play a bigger and bigger part in Norwich life, with explosive results (literally) the next century. But that's another story.

Kett's Rebellion

The most revolting revolt of them all...
...took place in June 1549, just a couple of years after young Edward VI became king. Edward, you'll remember, was surrounded by a group of rich and powerful nobles.

And it was the chief one, Lord Protector the Duke of Somerset, who helped spark Norfolk's biggest-ever revolt.

But he didn't mean to.

Meet Mr Kett
It happened like this. The peasants had been moaning for ages about the way landowners kept fencing off bits of common land to put their sheep and cattle on.

The peasants needed those pieces of land for their own livestock. But the landowners were the landowners and no-one dared argued with them.

Until, that is, Norfolk peasants heard that the country's number one Big Cheese, the Lord Protector, thought that, yes, the landowners were being unfair.

Well, that was all the encouragement the peasants needed. They gathered together at Hethersett and broke down fences belonging to an unpopular landowner called Flowerdew. And they were about to knock down the fences of another landowner, a Wymondham tanner called Robert Kett, when something remarkable happened.

He *joined* them. And quickly became their leader.

March on a fine city
Soon hundreds of angry peasants joined the rioters. They wanted their problems sorted out, and they wanted them sorted out NOW. And the best place to get that done was just up the road – at Norwich.

So they marched on the city.

Of course, by now the authorities had got wind of what was going on. Sir Edmund Windham, High Sheriff of Norfolk, rode out to Bowthorpe to meet the mob.

Their conversation was along these lines:

Sir Edmund: 'Look here you peasant chappies, you'd better jolly well go back to your villages unless…. Er, gulp, why are you waving those pitchforks at me?'

The Peasants replied: 'Grrrrrrrrr!!!!'

Sir Edmund only escaped by having a very fast horse.

Hmm, said the city officials. Time for plan B.

Plan B

At Hellesdon Bridge, a local magistrate met the mob (which was even bigger by now) and brought cartloads of beer and food.

Their conversation went like this:

Magistrate: 'Now then – you peasants have been very, very naughty. But if you agree to go home you can have this nice beer and food…. Er, gulp, why are you looking at me like that?'

Peasants: 'GRRRR!!!'

But the magistrate's horse wasn't fast enough. He was grabbed and chucked into a ditch.

83

The rebels' camp

By July 12 the rebel army set up camp on Mousehold Heath, where, of course, they could see exactly what was going on in the city.

From around 2000 the army grew to 16,000 as more peasants came from all over Norfolk.

Kett and his supporters drew up a list of 27 complaints, which were mostly about rotten landlords.

By now the Lord Protector was being pressed by the other nobles to stop supporting the peasants. He sent a messenger to try to sort out a peaceful end to the rebellion.

The fighting begins

But Kett rejected the call on July 21. The Norwich citizens shut all the city gates (which must have done them a fat lot of good since Mousehold Heath overlooked a big bit of the city which never had walls in the first place).

That night both sides fired their cannons.

The next day the rebels smashed their way into the city at Bishopgate (near the cathedral) and took over the city, grabbing the Mayor and other top officials as hostages.

The people of Norwich appealed for help to London. By August 1 the Marquis of Northampton had arrived with 1400 men (the rebels had 20,000, you'll remember).

But while the soldiers slept that night, the crafty rebels attacked and fought a bitter battle for three hours.

The next day they managed to break into the city across the river meadows.

A battle was fought in which the Government troops were defeated – and a noble (Lord Sheffield) killed. The rebels looted and burned part of the city. In fact one historian later reckoned only a big helping of rain saved Norwich from burning down.

The Government couldn't let this go on.

And they didn't.

A bum idea

By August 23 a fresh army – now 13,000 strong – had arrived under the command of the Earl of Warwick. The next day they sent a herald to talk to the rebels one last time. But his peace mission ended in laughter – and tragedy.

The laughter? A boy in Kett's army bared his bum at the Royal messenger. And the tragedy? One of the Earl's army was so disgusted he shot the boy ...dead. After that the Earl drove the rebels out of the city after bitter fighting at Elm Hill and around St Andrew's Hall.

The following morning Kett and his army tried and failed to get control of the city. On August 26 the rebels came down from their camp on Mousehold and met Warwick's army at Dussindale (probably somewhere near Sprowston Road).

The Battle of Dussindale

One of the odd things about the battle was that many of the peasants believed in a strange old rhyme which said:

'The country gnoffes [folk], Hob, Dick and Hick,
With clubs and clouted shoon [hob-nailed boots],
Shall fill the vale
Of Dussindale
With slaughtered bodies soon'

But when Warwick's expert cavalry charged the peasants, it became clear that the 'slaughtered bodies' were going to be the rebels themselves.

'Kett hiding is the last straw!'

It was soon over. The rebels broke and fled, with Warwick offering a pardon for the last few who resisted. Kett escaped but was caught in a barn at Swannington.

Remember the last city riot, Gladman's rebellion of 1463? Not one person had died in that. But at least 3000 died in this one.

And the killing wasn't over yet.

A terrible revenge

Robert Kett was executed and his body left hanging in a gibbet (metal cage) at Norwich Castle for months (there's a memorial to him there now). His brother was hanged too, along with the other ringleaders.

Kett's Rebellion had won its place in history. But at a terrible price.

PS Tradition has it the Cow Tower was hit by cannon fire during the revolt and still shows traces of burning on top.

PPS The Earl of Surrey's posh house, Mount Surrey on St Leonard's Hill, was one of the biggest casualties of the revolt. But the Earl, a poet and son of the Duke of Norfolk, was not upset. He wasn't around to do anything.

You see, he had made the mistake two years earlier of jumping the gun when Henry VIII lay dying. He dropped the hint that he would make a jolly good king when old Henry popped his clogs.

He even started using King Edward the Confessor's symbols on his coat of arms ('Hey, look at me everybody, I'm ROYAL!').

The trouble was, Henry might be dying – but he could still sign death warrants.

On January 19 1547 Surrey lost his head...

...for using the wrong arms.

Tudor Rich... and Poor

That's rich

Despite all the fighting, fires, religious strife and other disasters, Norwich in Tudor times was a happening place. Its trading position close to mainland Europe and its weaving and wool industry brought plenty of prosperity.

According to a survey, in 1524 Norwich was already three times richer than Lynn, and six times richer than Yarmouth – and those towns weren't slow when it came to making money.

Of course, everyone wanted a share of that wealth. We've already seen how farmworkers were even abandoning the harvest so they could come to the city and make money.

All these rural families – and the Strangers, of course – flocking to the city meant that Norwich's population almost doubled between 1520 and 1620 up to perhaps 20,000.

And that was despite thousands of people being killed by plague. It was the biggest city outside London – and stayed that way right up to the 18th century. But if you thought the wealth was shared out equally, you're in for a nasty surprise...

The haves...

A survey of the city accounts from 1525 showed that just 29 men owned more than a third of Norwich's wealth. Rich families made sure they were elected to important positions – and passed laws about things like trading to make sure they got even richer.

PROPERTY OF NORWICH

Over the Tudor period just 11 families dominated Norwich politics - the Anguishes, Ferrors, Barretts, Davies, Layers, Sucklings, Aldriches, Mingays, Pettus, Sothertons and Hyrnes. Between them they produced 31 generations of aldermen (city councillors) and 28 mayors.

For them life was prosperous, comfortable and really... rather nice.

...The have nots

For most people, of course, it was a very different story.

Often in history poor people tend to be 'invisible' when it comes to having their story told.

Only the deeds of rich and powerful royalty, nobles and churchmen were thought worth recording.

Ordinary people – like peasants – were just there to work... and behave.

But Norwich is different.

It is different because it has a large amount of city records – and especially a huge 1570 survey of the poor people in the city – which tell some fascinating stories.

And plenty of sad ones too.

The story of Robert Browne

Young Robert Browne came to Norwich from his home in Suffolk in 1559 to find a better life. He was aged about 12, but wasn't sure.

The better life was hard to find. He grew steadily weaker with hunger until one day he just collapsed in the street.

And that was when his luck changed. Robert Saborne, who lived around Muspole Street, found him and – as the records put it – 'being moved with pity' took him home and gave him food, clothes and shelter.

He promised the city authorities that when the boy reached the age of 14 he would take him on as an apprentice to learn his trade of weaving.

That was a sad story with a happy ending. But how many others like young Robert just stayed in the gutter? We will never know.

Begging for a change

The city authorities, as we've seen, took begging very seriously. It wasn't just the numbers of the beggars that worried them – it was the growing fear that beggars might join in any riot which happened to be going on.

Or even start their own for the sheer fun of it.

The city even bought Bridewell as a 'house of correction' where beggars could be locked up or forced to work.

The city records have plenty of reports about how beggars were dealt with (usually whipped and chucked out of the city gates).

'Beggars can't be choosers"

Bringing the poor to their Census

A huge Census – survey – in 1570 tried to find out exactly how many poor there were in the city, who they were, and where they lived.

The document is a fantastic picture of what sort of lives almost 2400 of the poorest people in Norwich lived more than 400 years ago. And, amazingly, it was only re-discovered in its complete state in 1962.

In late 1570 the mayor, John Aldrich, started a big campaign against beggars. He said that the 'foolish pity' of the merchants meant beggars were being given so much free food and other goodies that other poor people were giving up their jobs and going begging instead.

But the survey was hardly about beggars at all, but 790 poor families.

The real reason for the survey took place on May 16 that year, when John Appleyard and Brian Holland tried to start a revolt against the Strangers. That effort failed, but worried everyone that unless the poor of the city were given a better deal, they could well join the next uprising.

After all, when you have nothing, what is there to lose?

The survey looked at the poorest families in Norwich. And showed how desperate some of them were. There were families so poor that they had to live in the cold and draughty old gatehouses and towers on the city walls because they couldn't afford a proper house.

And children were working (usually at weaving) from four years old.

Being poor in 1570
Here's some typical entries from the big Census:

*Ann Buck, 46, widow, sousster [sauce maker] and teaches children, and has two children, one aged nine, and the other aged five who works lace.... very poor

*William Carter, 22, diseased of a sore leg and is without comfort... very poor.

*Michael Maste, 26, blacksmith out of work, and Suzan, his wife of the same age, very sick... very poor

About one in ten of the adults were sick or disabled in some way, with one in four of over 60s likely to be severely disabled.

Almost 370 women were living on their own, with 46 having been deserted by their husbands. Like mother-of-one Margaret Clason, 41, whose mason husband John had left her nine years earlier.

She was yet another one the survey said was 'very poor'.

It also showed people were crammed into properties. Two houses in St Benedict's had 16 people living in them, while a Mrs Croke even had a house with 25 people in it.

And who were the slum landlords who were filling their houses with the poor, and so worrying the city aldermen no end? Why, in many cases, the city aldermen themselves...

What happened next
The Orders for the Poor were the city's response.

It was determined to stop cases of beggars being found in house doorways. As their report said: 'So cared they not for apparel [clothes] though the cold struck so deeply into them, that what with diseases and want of changing their clothes their flesh was eaten with vermin and corrupt diseases grew upon them...'

Yuck. Just as bad, they said, were the ones who spent all day in the pub instead of working.

Something had to be done!

Here's what they decided:

1 Caught begging? You'll be whipped six times.

2 Caught giving food to beggars? You'll be fined four pence (about 2p) every time.

3 To appoint two officers ('deacons') in each district to deal with the poor.

4 To set up a special house for men and women to work.

'And I promise I'll be good...if you just let me win the Lottery'

5 Twelve people to be kept there as prisoners for 21 days (at least). And if they didn't work, they'd be whipped – and kept hungry until they *did* work.

And they really made them work hard. They got up at 5am in summer and worked until 8pm at night, with 30 minutes to have something to eat – and another 15 minutes praying (to win the Tudor version of the National Lottery, we expect).

If all this sounds pretty nasty, then just think that these rules were way ahead of what other cities and towns could offer. It's hard to believe, but Norwich was actually a *kinder* place to live than just about anywhere else in the country.

Poor end to the century

All these surveys, all these changes, all those laws, didn't stop people wanting to come to Norwich for a better life.

An account book from 1600 or so shows cases such as an eight-year-old girl – yes, *eight* – travelling from Staffordshire to Norwich (240km!), and an 11-year-old coming all the way from London.

Both wanted the chance for a new life. Both were whipped and sent back home instead.

The rich were still rich. And the poor were still poor.

Some things never changed.

The Savage Stuarts

Religious rumpus

You might have thought all the bloodshed, fighting and assorted nastiness over religion in the Tudor period would have been enough.

Sadly, it wasn't.

Extreme Protestants – Puritans – gradually started to take control of the city. This had worried Queen Elizabeth, you'll remember, and soon brought the city into conflict with the Bishop of Norwich (again!).

What started as a row over what direction the Church of England should take got caught up in the much bigger dispute between the Stuart kings and Parliament in the 1630s and 1640s. And all that ended in the biggest nastiness of the century – the English Civil War.

The pushy Puritans

The Puritans thought their 'pure' type of religion was the best. They hated people having, well, any fun at all (even Christmas). Some left for the new colonies in America in the 1620s and 30s (including a former Norwich apprentice Samuel Lincoln in 1637. One of his descendants was President Abraham Lincoln).

Meanwhile, here in Norwich, things were hotting up...

Here's how the row got bigger:

In 1622 Bishop Harsnett bans Sunday morning sermons and lectures to try to stop the Puritans.

1623: Three hundred sign a protest petition about the ban...

1630s: Puritan preaching flourishes in such churches as St Peter Hungate...

1635: Bishop Matthew Wren takes over - and immediately launches another crackdown on the pesky Puritans.

Wren made life so uncomfortable for the Puritans that some preachers took exile in Holland (which is strange because two generations earlier the Strangers had taken exile from Holland to Norwich for their beliefs. The wheel had turned full circle...).

Service with a snarl

And then the city corporation - full of Puritans - was ordered by King Charles I to attend the cathedral every Sunday for the service.

The whole service - all three to four hours of it!

The city officials said: 'But it's too long - and too cold in winter'.

But they were told: 'Ha, ha - tough luck. You'd better get used to it!'

So, grumbling, they did what they were told. But they weren't happy.

They were even unhappier when they realised that they were forced to sit under an overhanging gallery.

Soon people were taking advantage by dropping books, stools, shoes and hats on them, cutting up their gowns and even - wait for it - *weeing* and *pooing* on their heads while they were praying!

The aldermen and their wives were furious at being humiliated.

One day soon, they said, we'll get our own back....

In 1639 Wren's successor told Charles I that the area was 'as quiet, uniform, and comfortable as any in the kingdom, if not more...'

Er, oh no it wasn't!

The Great Fire of Norwich (Nearly)

If all this wasn't enough religious rowing, in November 1641 two Catholics tried to burn Norwich down by setting fires at each end. Or at least that's what a pamphlet printed in London a few days later claimed. It had the snappy title: 'Bloody News from Norwich; or, A True Relation of a bloody attempt of the Papists in Norwich to Consume the Whole City by Fire.'

But the real anger was still between the Puritan city and the Dean and Chapter...

The coming of war

The Puritan Parliament was getting ready to raise an army against the king. This encouraged the Puritans of Norwich. In February 1642 a mob threatened to storm the cathedral and destroy some of the 'papist' (Roman Catholic) images there. But the Dean and Chapter removed some of the fittings to head off the riot. It worked – that time.

The national King v Parliament dispute finally reached Norwich on July 28 1642. Captain Treswell appeared in the city with orders for 100 volunteers to go and help the king. But the city had him arrested instead – and sent him to Parliament. Now there was no turning back for Norwich.

King Charles appealed to the city for help in late August – and was ignored. Instead, the city set to work repairing the old walls and had plans to build an earth bank to defend the Wensum from attack.

In January 1643 the Mayor, William Gostlyn – a Royalist – was sent to jail. Any supporters of the king were thrown off the city authority.

In March the rebels' leader, Oliver Cromwell, stopped off in Norwich (nipping over to Lowestoft to crush a Royalist revolt on the way, as you do). And – hint, hint – he made sure he arrived on the same day of the city elections.

The Puritans' revenge
Sooner or later, the powerful Puritans were going to get their own back on the cathedral. And in November 1643, they did.

An armed mob led by two aldermen broke into the cathedral. The damage was terrible – they smashed stained glass, burnt religious items, church clothes and hymn books.

We have a grim eyewitness account of the rampaging mob.

Bishop Hall wrote: 'What clattering of glass! What beating down of walls! What tearing up of monuments! What pulling down of seats! What wresting out of irons and brass from the windows and graves! What defacing of arms! What demolishing of the curious stone-work...!'

He added: 'The cathedral was filled with musketeers [soldiers] drinking and tobacconing [smoking] as freely as if it had been turned into an alehouse.' The mob carried what they could find to the market – where they burned it to cheers and shouts.

It's amazing anything survived. You can still see a musket ball stuck in the tomb of Bishop Goldwell. Happily, the beautiful roof bosses (one of the wonders of Norwich Cathedral) were too high up to damage, and a medieval painted wooden panel was rediscovered in 1847. It had been used as a table for centuries – until someone looked underneath...

Other churches in Norwich were also ransacked. The accounts for St Lawrence's in 1643 show a Goodman Perfitt was paid 1s 8d (about 9p) for 'putting out the superstitious inscriptions on the church windows and the pulling down of crucifixes'. The following year saw religious statues from the cathedral, St Swithin's and St Peter Mancroft piled up in the market place – and burned.

How the Cathedral itself survived after Cromwell took power is a bit of a miracle. Lead was stolen from the roof, and the town of Great Yarmouth even asked Cromwell that the 'great useless pile, the cathedral, might be pulled down and the stones given them to build a workhouse'.

Riot, 'The Great Blowe' – and hailstones!
It would have been nice if Norwich had had a bit of peace and quiet for the next few years. But, hey, this is Nasty Norwich we are talking about – and there were plenty of calamities round the corner.

'We're hungry for a change in the rotten old tax!"

In December 1646 there were riots again. It was not politics or religion which sparked them this time – but empty bellies. The poor were furious at excise duties [taxes] being put on their meat and ale. The rioting spread into the countryside before being stopped.

And history took an explosive turn in April 1648 when Norwich was shaken – literally – by the most violent incident in the city over the Civil War period.

And it's an incident we have no fewer than 278 witnesses' stories about.

It all started like this: in 1647-8 the mayor was John Utting. John was a Royalist, which as you can expect made him very unpopular among the Puritans. In April 1648 they asked Parliament for the power to remove him, which caused dismay among the mayor's supporters.

On April 23 word got round that Utting was to be arrested.

A crowd of 2000 broke into the house of Puritan Thomas Ashwell and stole weapons.

They then marched on the Committee House (at the site of the later Bethel hospital) where Norfolk's guns and armour were kept.

Someone fired a gun from inside the building, killing a boy. Furious, the mob burst into the building, gunpowder got spilled, someone made a spark and...

...80 barrels of gunpowder exploded, destroying the building, killing 40 people and blowing out the windows of St Peter Mancroft and St Stephen's Church among much other damage.

Just how much damage it caused can be guessed from the fact that when Guy Fawkes and his friends plotted to blow up Parliament they were going to use 36 barrels!

The rioters were caught by Colonel Fleetwood's troopers, and at court sessions in December 66 were charged. Eight were hanged in the Castle Ditch on January 2 1649 (we sincerely hope someone didn't wish them 'Happy New Year' the day before), and the rest were jailed, fined – or both.

Meanwhile, in London, Charles I was also not celebrating the New Year because later that month he, too, was executed. Cromwell and his cronies had won. What did the city assembly do? It sent Cromwell a message of congratulation.

That didn't stop the Royalists from plotting, though.

In the same year 24 people in Norfolk were tried for plotting, with some being hung in Norwich as well as other Norfolk towns. And in 1655 the Royalists tried again to revolt, putting Norwich in a panic. But that didn't work either.

If civil war wasn't bad enough, Nature wanted to have a go too.

On July 20 1656 there was one of the worst storms in the city's history. A pamphlet of the time spoke of 'the loud claps from the clouds so amazed the people that they thought the spheres [planets] came thundering down in flames about their ears.'

Hailstones bigger than oranges came crashing into the city with reports of every single window facing south and south-east being shattered.

It was another rotten blow for Norwich... but a profitable one for people who sold glass.

By 1658, when Cromwell died, the people were growing tired of Puritan rule.

Cromwell's son Richard took over for a couple of years, but Charles II was unstoppable.

And when the army declared they would support the king in May 1660, Norwich city assembly – the same people, you'll recall, who'd cheered when Charles I had had his head chopped off – sent a message of congratulations to their new king.

Two-faced? How could you even *think* such a thing!

You might think that riots, war, executions, destruction and explosions would be enough nastiness for one century.

But – guess what – you'd be wrong!

Sickly Stuarts

There was plenty of other nastiness going on in Stuart Norwich. Here's just some of it...

The deadly visitor

At the start of the 17th century Norwich was a thriving place. Its population was about 14,000, with thousands of immigrants from the Low Countries boosting the city's weaving industry.

And then the plague came back. Between August 1603 and July 1604 about a quarter of those city folk died in one year.

But still the city grew and grew. By 1620 the population was up to about 22,000 - with almost everyone living within the city walls.

This meant that the population (which had now doubled in 20 years) had to scrap for whatever room they could find.

You'll remember that by 1570 it was so crowded that the poor were having to sleep in the old towers on the walls. Well, by the 1620s more and more people were being crammed into smelly courts and yards off the main streets. There were 70 living in one tenement at St Martin-at-Palace alone!

'Hmmm... only room for another 20, then...'

It's no surprise that plague kept coming back. Between 1625 and 1626 up to a quarter of the population perished in yet another outbreak.

The city authorities were so desperate to stop the disease spreading that they slaughtered just about every animal they could grab. Dogs, cats and even doves were killed.

Smelly Stuarts

The place still stank too. The only things that changed about the poo supply was that:

1.   There was twice as much as there had been in Tudor times. Twice the people = twice the poo!

2.   People were using chamber pots instead of digging holes in the ground.

But when the chamber pots were full, the contents were just chucked out in the street, as usual. Looking up to check for windows being opened by poo chuckers was as important as watching where you trod.

Remember all those laws they kept passing in medieval Norwich about piles of poo in the streets? Things were still rotten in 1686 because new bylaws ordered yet another clean-up. The reason? So much dirt and filth were being washed into the Wensum that it was getting in the way of the boats.

'That's the last time I go for a swim in there!'

Fancy a dip, anyone?

The Great Plague

When plague swept through London in 1665, killing perhaps 100,000 people out of 500,000, the rest of Britain trembled. They knew that unless they were very, very lucky, it would be their turn next.

Norwich was more worried than most. For a start, it had suffered terrible outbreaks of plague every decade or so for almost a hundred years.

And then there was the fact that Great Yarmouth started reporting cases (blamed on a Dutch trading ship) from as early as November 1664.

The city authorities tried stopping boats from Yarmouth outside the city boundaries and ordering them to be unloaded in open country. For a while it worked. But by September 1665 plague had come back to haunt Norwich.

By early summer in 1666 the numbers dying had started to grow alarmingly. The town clerk Thomas Corie wrote that 'the plague grows fast among us, and poverty faster.'

He was worried that the cost of giving emergency help to the poor meant the city would soon run out of money. It didn't help that all the posh people left the city as soon as they could, leaving the poor people to suffer the brunt of the disease.

By late August 203 people a week were dying of plague - and the city had run out of money. With food running short, Corie was terrified the starving poor would rampage through the streets.

But the city was saved by... a big shoal of fish. Yarmouth fishermen found a huge stock of herring so that by September Corie could record 'twelve herring a penny here fills many an empty belly'.

By the time the plague stopped in early June 1667, more than 2800 people had died, perhaps a fifth of the population.

Most people died in the poorest districts. In fact

'When I said I didn't want fish for supper again, they told me to stop carping...'

you were *three* times as likely to end up with the plague if you were poor.

But at least this was the last outbreak of plague to hit the city.

A grim reminder of its cost came almost 130 years later. In February 1796 some labourers were digging in a field at Lakenham when they came across nearly a hundred human skulls and other bones, buried just 25cm underground. A copper coin dating from 1664 showed that this was almost certainly some of the victims of Norwich's 1665-7 plague outbreak.

A deadly new visitor
Although plague came to an end with this outbreak, there was another killer waiting just round the corner... SMALLPOX.

The disease was the most feared illness of the late 17th century and for a hundred years after that. Norwich was swept by an outbreak from 1669-70, killing 300 families in just a fortnight. The town clerk wrote: 'The smallpox rageth still amongst us, and poverty daily invades us like an armed man.'

King Charles' nasty surprise
When Charles II visited the city in September 1671 there was, as you might expect, great joy all around. The city presented him with 200 guineas (£210) which must have pleased him.
But what they showed him next would have wiped the smile straight off his face.

'Stone me, what a rotten present!'

It was an enormous stone which had been extracted - without anaesthetic! - from someone's bladder (the part of the body where wee is stored).

Lots of Norfolk people used to suffer from this extremely painful condition, which was thought to be linked to poor diet.

It wasn't the king's first encounter with the medical conditions of Norwich.

In March 1668 the city sent Sarah Hunter to London to be touched by the king.

You see, she had the extremely nasty condition known as scrofula or 'the king's evil', which produced some yukky skin growths. The only cure was supposed to be having the infection touched by the king or queen.

So it wasn't all fun being the monarch!

The story of the Disappearing Palace

Charles stayed in the Palace of the Duke of Norfolk while he was in Norwich.

Its story is one of the saddest in the whole nasty Norwich saga.

Back in 1540 the Duke of the day built a palace as his town residence. It was the largest private house in the city and stood between Duke Street and St Andrew's Street. It was up to four storeys high with gardens, a covered tennis court and a bowling alley.

'And for my next trick I'll make my palace disappear!'

Thomas Howard, the 4th Duke, boasted that his house was worth only a little less than the *whole* of Scotland!

He spent £30,000 on doing it up - equal to zillions in today's money.

But that was nothing compared to the Duke's Palace version 2.0 which replaced it in 1602.

The original was demolished and rebuilt to make was what claimed to be most lavish building in the country which didn't belong to the monarch.

A third version of the palace was completed in 1672 - but there is not a scrap to be seen today.

Why? It was all because the city mayor, Thomas Havers, refused permission in 1710 for the Duke to have his company of players march into Norwich with trumpets sounding. You see, Havers was terrified that the procession would be used as an excuse by fellow Roman Catholics (the Howards still kept to their original faith) for a riot or even worse.

But the Duke was so furious that he demolished most of the palace in spite. Only one wing survived as a workhouse. And when that vanished there was just the old Roman Catholic chapel left.

That survived until the 1960s - as a billiard room! It was pulled down to make room for the multi-storey car park.

Now only the names Duke Street and Duke's Palace Bridge are reminders of the days when Norwich held one of the poshest houses in England.

That's entertainment?

Marching processions were just one of the ways the good folk of Norwich kept themselves amused. Other favourite 17th century pastimes included nine-pin bowling, which sounds quite pleasant.

But they also loved freak shows, which were most definitely not nice.

Anybody who was unusual could find themselves paraded at one of the local pubs. Giants were very popular (one woman was 2.25m tall), as were people born without arms or hands, or especially hairy. One child exhibited had six fingers on each hand.

Animals, too, were put on parade. Imagine popping into your local and finding yourself looking at a lion - or a camel. It really happened in Norwich!

In 1675 someone even claimed to have put two mermaids on display.

Not surprisingly, perhaps, the pubs of Norwich had a reputation for being wild. In 1681 there were complaints that the city 'swarmed with alehouses' where you could buy the company of women.

It was too much beer at the Maid's Head in July 1684 which led to a sensational murder case. Thomas Burney (or Berney or Barney - the books differ) got drunk and ended up quarrelling with a Mr Bedingfield, who was later found stabbed.

Burney was hanged in Town Close for the crime.

Funnily enough, a French dancing master later confessed on his deathbed that he, not Burney, had stabbed the man...

The witch scares

In 1950 some houses near Horns Lane (off King Street) were being demolished when workmen discovered a hidden jar containing human hair, finger nails and iron nails.

It was a witch-bottle - put together by a worried householder in the 17th century to try to stop a witch's spell being put on him.

Belief in witches had been growing across Europe for centuries. Even kings and queens were concerned by it. While Queen Elizabeth was making her visit to Norwich in 1578, she was worried that wax figures (including one with her name on it) had been found in London.

'I'm hoping this will give me a spell of protection'

But that was nothing compared to what happened around 1645-6.

An extremely nasty lawyer from Essex, Matthew Hopkins, discovered he had a talent - he could terrorise old ladies into saying anything... even that they were witches.

He declared himself 'Witchfinder-General' and set off across Norfolk and Suffolk to 'find' witches (and be paid handsomely by grateful town councils).

He probably worked in Norwich too, because in July 1645 around 40 witches were tried at Norwich Assizes - even the 20 of them who had already been executed (now that's *really* nasty justice).

Even after horrible Hopkins had gone, 'witches' were still being found.

On January 2 1649, for instance, two of them - Anne Dant and Margaret Turrell - were hanged at the castle, after a trial that had been held on Christmas Day.

'...and so the court has decided to sentence you to death. Oh, and a merry Christmas.'

Even a clever person like Norwich's famous historian and naturalist Sir Thomas Browne (that's him in that statue on Hay Hill) was taken in.

Sir Thomas might have been smart enough to invent words like 'electricity' (or so it's claimed) and be praised across Europe for his great brain – but witches were definitely his weak spot.

He once went along to a trial at Bury St Edmunds where two women were accused of bewitching young children.

The judge thought the evidence was weak, but then spotted

the Smartest Man in Norwich in the gallery and asked his opinion. 'Oh, guilty, of course!' came the reply. They were hanged.

The Orange riots
When Charles II died in 1685, his brother James came to the throne - and tried to make England a Roman Catholic country again.

But James was forced to flee the country in 1688 when Royal rivals William of Orange (chosen because he was 'a-peeling' and had a thick skin, I suppose) and his wife Mary arrived in the country from Holland with an army.

In November 1688 mobs rioted in Norwich in support of the Protestant William and Mary, destroying a Catholic chapel and threatening the cathedral and bishop's palace.

On December 1 the Duke of Norfolk and 300 knights and gentlemen rode into the city.

They declared William king. But the trouble didn't end there: In March 1689 a mob gathered and threatened to attack the bishop's palace - they thought James II was hiding inside!

Growing pains
Despite all the century's fighting, plague, smallpox and other nasty incidents, the population of Norwich was still growing fast. By 1693 it stood at an estimated 28,881, the second largest city in the country (Bristol in comparison only had 19,400 people).

And nine-tenths of those were still jammed together within the city walls.

So, what nastiness would the new century hold? Let's go and find out, shall we...

The Grisly Georgians

Street life

Visitors to Norwich often described it two different ways.

There were those who looked on the bright side and saw all the trees in places like Chapelfield and described Norwich as a 'city in an orchard, or an orchard in a city' - but for many others it was a smelly place with cramped, dirty streets. An Act of Parliament in 1700 (followed by another 11 years later) tried to make sure the streets were at least lit, but it stayed a city of contrasts throughout the century.

There were many fine houses and gardens, but there were some awful slums, especially near the river. It didn't help the poor people that the Wensum was always at risk of flooding (there were big floods in 1763 and 1770, for instance). Then there was the pong and other dangers - which included falling in the river when going for a wee.

And Norwich got more and more cramped... by 1714 there were around 30,000 people, by 1771 that was up to 36,000 (making Norwich still the third biggest city in the country) and by the end of the century it had reached almost 40,000.

Almost all of these people were housed within the old city walls.

By 1783 the city authorities had this to say about Norwich's streets: 'Persons on foot must squeeze themselves into a dark alley, or burst into a shop to avoid being run over or crushed against the walls, while in wet weather, you are drenched by torrents of water from the houses, or plunged into a gutter, knee deep.'

One sad effect of all this overcrowding was the decision between 1791 and 1810 to take down all of Norwich's medieval gates to help the traffic flow. The city bosses also reckoned it would make the air pass easier and stop nasty diseases (wrong!).

Quirky fact: They missed one bit!

Part of St Benedict's Gates survived right up until April 1942 - when a Nazi warplane dropped a bomb on it. Not even its most far-sighted builders could have predicted *that*.

Putrid pubs

Lots of nasty things could happen in Norwich's horrible pubs. Even murder. In 1701 a jealous weaver called Robert Watts, who was living at the Old Globe in Botolph Street, murdered his wife because he thought she had been too friendly with another man. He was hanged outside the pub. I bet that put the regulars off their beer.

A grim story? Yes, of course. But a good way of introducing a nasty side to Norwich - the awful pubs.

They were centres of gambling, crime, blood-letting, drunkenness and freak-shows.

And wee. For many city pubs had a chamber pot in the corner for the use of customers. It wasn't emptied until it was full - however long that took.

The drink on sale wasn't exactly cola or lemonade. Two notorious local brews were 'Norwich Nog' and the even more stronger 'Clamberskull'. One writer noted that 'if a man could drink a quart [about 1.1 litres] and walk through the door without touching the door-posts he was considered a seasoned toper [drinker]'.

DANGER! Drink at your peril!

And the landlords didn't exactly encourage responsible drinking.

The landlord of the Fountain in St Benedict's (funnily enough, another building destroyed in the April 1942 air raids) took out an advertisement in 1741 that anyone who owed him money could clear the debt by drinking the cost of it in beer.

The beer wasn't the only attraction. Landlords at many of the best inns had a room set aside as a cockpit, a narrow space where trained cockerels fought each other, while 'gentlemen' placed bets on the outcome.

So what other things could you see at Norwich's pubs?

Make your selection from this list... tigers, giants, leopards, ostriches, a whale, dwarfs, giants, fire-eaters and mermaids.

So which were actually shown at local pubs? They **ALL** were. Yes, even the whale! Taken at Wells, it was advertised as having 'given entire satisfaction to all who have seen it'.

One of the biggest drinking days in Norwich was on February 3 every year. That was the anniversary of Bishop Blaise, the patron saint of woolcombers.

It was the excuse for the city's weavers to take part in a procession, gamble at cards, dice and cock-fighting - and drink and drink and drink....

(Talking about bishops, it's hard to believe that even at this date there were FIVE pubs in Cathedral Close).

We started this section with death, so we'll end it that way too. In November 1787 there was a notorious case in one of Norwich's most famous pubs when Lamb Inn landlord John Aggas was murdered by his brother-in-law Timothy Hardy.

And the sad and lonely death of John Stimpson at the Bull in St Stephen's in 1794 is a reminder of another grim practice which was not abolished until 1823. If you took your own life (as poor Stimpson did) you were buried not in a churchyard, but at a crossroads - and with a stake through your heart...

Horrible hospitals
You might think it was the Victorians who first built modern hospitals. And you'd be wrong.

In 1772 the Norfolk and Norwich Hospital opened... and treated just three people on its first day (the modern-day version usually sees about 500 times as many every day).

You see, one of the main aims of the hospital seems to have been to keep sick people out! Rules from 1782 refused entry to heavily pregnant women, children under six, anyone 'disordered in their senses'

'Of course you can't come in - you're ill!'

or suffering from consumption [tuberculosis] or thought to have smallpox or 'the itch'.

Oh, and anyone who was dying or incurable either.

It's a wonder they managed to treat as many as three.

The Norfolk and Norwich tried to keep up to date with the latest medical advances.

It even ordered a machine in 1787 for giving healthy electric shocks to patients!

The N and N was famous for its operations for removing stones from people's bladders (remember Charles II's nasty little surprise from the last chapter?). Amazingly, in an age when people didn't have anaesthetic (and no-one knew about germs), six out of seven people survived the operation.

And the hospital kept all the stones - and hundreds of others.

It still has a unique collection of 1500 bladder stones from operations from 1771 to 1909. Top medic Sir Henry Thompson liked it.

In 1863 he described the collection 'as the most perfect and complete record, literally graven in stone, that the world possesses of calculous experience'. But we'd rather go YEEEEUCK! if you don't mind!

113

The medical museum also included, at one stage, a skeleton of a dwarf executed at Norwich Castle for murder - and the skull of good old Sir Thomas ('I spy with my little eye something beginning with W') Browne.

As well as keeping out the really ill, the authorities were also determined that no-one should come out of hospital the tiniest bit well-fed. In 1785 the Governors asked the doctors and surgeons 'to determine whether the [food] allowance is not too much, as a large quantity of bread and other provisions were found concealed in the wards upon a search made'.

It's out of the 18th century but we can't resist this bit: in 1823 the father of a young boy whose leg had been amputated turned up with an unusual request... could he have the leg back please? No-one at the hospital was quite sure what he wanted to do with it, but he was too late anyway - it had been buried.

If all this sounds horrible, we should point out that Norwich was one of the first places in the country (1713) to build a hospital - the Bethel - for people with mental health problems.

Rows and riots

Now, where would Norwich be without a few good riots?

We've seen over the centuries how the good folk of Norwich liked nothing better than a bit of civic unrest.

So here's our top five Riots of the 18th Century...

At number **FIVE**..... Riots over Stuarts: On August 20 1714 - the coronation day of George I - there were attacks on the homes of people who supported the exiled Stuart King James.

The subject prompted another riot two years later.

(Nasty footnote: Talking of Stuart plots, in 1722 Norwich lawyer Christopher Layer got caught up in various hare-brained ideas for putting James III on the throne. He was caught, convicted - and then hung, drawn and quartered. Not nice.)

At number **FOUR**.... Riots over Trade: On December 13 1720 a mob in Pockthorpe (then one of the poorest areas of the city, round where Barrack Street is now) raided shops selling calicoes, a type of imported cloth.

They were so angry that trade was being taken away from local weavers that they even tore calico dresses off the backs of women in the streets!

At number **THREE**…. Riots over Food: In 1740 there were two riots about it.

One group protested about not

'This foreign cloth is a rip-off!'

having enough grain, going out into the countryside and demanding money and beer from farmers. Soldiers killed one of the rioters – and, er, seven innocent bystanders. And then there was the time they rioted about the price of fish... for *five* days!

At number **TWO**… Riots over Religion. Not Protestant v Catholic this time, but over the new Christian group the Methodists in 1751-2. A mob of up to 10,000 got involved in big fights over Methodist preacher James Wheatley, who was, according to a diary at the time, 'shamefully handled, his hat and wig lost, his head broken in several places...' A group of rebellious and rich young men called the Hell-Fire Club were behind a lot of the trouble. They used to meet at the Blue Bell on Orford Hill.

And the chart-topper, at number **ONE**… A riot over, well, everything really. In September 1766 a huge mob destroyed market place stalls, houses, and partly demolished the White Horse in the Haymarket.

Two of the rioters were executed and four others transported for life to our American colonies. It was the worst riot of the century.

115

Transport problem

Talking about transportation, Norwich was involved right from the word go with the new settlement of Australia. The Government thought that by shipping criminals halfway round the world - known as 'transportation' - it would be an excellent way of getting rid of Britain's crime problem by passing it to the other side of the world to sort out.

Norwich jail was where criminals from around the area were kept until the fleet of prison ships was ready to take the first group of prisoners in 1786.

They included Henry Cabell, convicted of burglary and stuck in jail since 1783, and Susannah Holmes, who had been convicted in the same year of the same crime. They met in Norwich jail, fell in love and had a son in 1786. Susannah and her baby were ordered to go to Plymouth to catch the ships - but Henry Cabell had to plead with the Home Secretary of the day to be allowed to go too.

They were married on February 10 1788 - one of the first couples ever to get married in Australia. They went on to become one of Australia's most famous 'First Fleet' families.

But for most of the 500-plus criminals who followed in their footsteps from Norwich jail the story didn't have such a happy ending.

The boy who out-Mozarted Mozart

Mozart was the most famous young musical genius of all time.

The Austrian composer was writing amazing pieces of music when just a small child. And he played before George III aged just seven years old.

But a Norwich composer played before the king aged THREE! And William Crotch was able to play 'God Save the King' when he was just two.

Other amazing things he could do was tell what the notes were when 12 keys were pressed down at the same time. Another party trick was writing with his right hand, then his left and then *backwards* with his left hand.

Our William was a bit unlucky though. He managed to stab himself with a toy soldier, break his collar bone in a coach accident, fall off a ladder - and then nearly fall down a coal cellar. Not all on the same day though!

'Thank goodness nothing else can go wrong!'

Sadly he's almost forgotten nowadays - perhaps it's because 'William Crotch' doesn't quite sound as glamorous as 'Wolfgang Amadeus Mozart'.

But it's believed that William - who was known as 'The Musical Child' - did leave us with one of the most famous pieces of music in the world, the Westminster Chimes. That's the tune that Big Ben makes before it goes BONG! - and it's been copied by millions of clocks all over the world. Even Mozart never managed that. So there!

Talking about bells, St Peter Mancroft has a world claim to fame of its own. On May 2 1715 its ringers performed a complicated feat of bell-ringing called Gransir Bob Triples. It was the first true 'peal of bells' ever and involved 5050 lots of ringing. That's a lot of aching arms – and an awful lot of disturbed snoozes!

The Wild Man of Norwich
You've seen the Wild Man pub sign in Bedford Street. But do you know the story behind it? The pub is supposed to be named after Peter the Wild Boy, who was found living with wild animals by George I while hunting in Germany. Peter was brought back to England to be educated but escaped.

When he arrived in Norwich he couldn't speak - so they stuck him in jail in the Bridewell as a vagrant. When the Bridewell caught fire in 1751 the prisoners were released - and the city jailer suddenly realised exactly who the mysterious vagrant was.

Peter went back to his teacher and lived until 1785.

Looming disaster

You'll remember that Norwich had become very rich because of its weaving trade.

It was famous for a type of cloth called 'worsted' (named after the village of Worstead) and Norfolk man Robert Walpole (Britain's first Prime Minister) tried to help the trade as much as he could.

The city weavers were very keen to keep their trade on top - and outsiders out.

We've seen how they rioted in 1720, and in 1752 they went on strike - and won - because of an apprentice they didn't like.

Almost everyone seemed to be involved in the wool trade in some way, from the women and children who prepared the wool thread, to the men who weaved it on looms in thousands of city attics, to the merchants and traders who sold the cloth.

But trouble was just around the corner.

Norwich had a lot going for it - it was the centre of a big region and had a cheap and skilled workforce.

But it was a long way from big centres of population (it took a day for even the fastest coach to to get to London) - and had no coal and no iron.

In 1753 a diarist wrote: 'This is a distressing time for Norwich, our manufacturers are nearly all at a stand still... no demand, no orders and no probability of any coming.' Norwich got through that crisis, but by 1771 the worsted trade was declining - partly blamed on the growing trouble with our American colonies.

But even by 1791 Norwich woollens were still worth a whopping £1 million-plus every year.

But Yorkshire factory owners were quickly starting to pinch Norwich's trade. They had built machines which could weave much faster - and cheaper - than Norwich's weavers could by hand.

The war with France in the 1790s was another big blow to local weavers. When William Windham, a politician in favour of the war, was elected MP in 1794, his angry opponents held a procession and claimed the trade would soon die.

Norwich needed to find a new way of staying wealthy - and fast!

The Nasty Nineteenth Century

A slice of the future

Remember those fish pies that Norwich was supposed to send to the king every year? When do you think the custom died out? 1327? 1458? 1515? It's amazing but the last pies were only sent in 1816!

Why are we telling you this? Well, apart from being a good mini-fact, it shows that Norwich was really still pretty much a medieval city at heart. Thousands of the houses were the same as in Tudor and Stuart times, and most people still lived within the old city walls. And the chief industry was still weaving - as it had been for hundreds of years.

In just a few decades, though, just about everything that goes to make up modern-day Norwich was begun: proper roads, railway stations, suburbs, gas supplies, electricity, decent sewers (hooray!), new industries, theatres, a police force, modern schools (boo!) - even the first time (1825) that people were supposed to drive on the left...

And the population almost tripled in number.

But before all that progress could arrive there was plenty of nastiness to put up with first!

Growing pains

By 1801 there were 36,909 people living in Norwich. This was the figure taken in the first proper 'Census', or people count. This count was to be held every ten years across the whole country (it still is) and gives us, at last, the number of how many people lived in certain years.

And they still wanted to come and live in Norwich! The big industrial cities like Manchester, Leeds and Birmingham might have loads more people by now, but people still flocked to the city - especially if (as often happened) there was no work or decent wages on farms and in the villages.

The population level stayed about where it was for ten years and then suddenly grew. By 1821 there were more than 50,000 people in the city. And that meant, at last, that people started living outside the old city walls (although there were thousands still crammed inside, as we'll see).

Builders started putting up street after street, estate after estate. In fact, so many streets went up that they ran out of street names and started using numbers. So you could well end up living in a house on Nineteen Row, for example.

What were these houses like? In many cases, terrible. There were almost 11,000 houses in 1821 Norwich - up 2300 (almost a quarter) in just ten years. Even with all the new areas being built on, there was still massive overcrowding.

Now, was it 19 Twenty Street – or 20 Nineteen Street?'

So what was life like for people living there? Let's see, shall we. But be warned, it doesn't make for pretty reading...

Being poor

If you were at the bottom of the heap life could be terrible. Remember the Duke of Norfolk's Palace? The building, which had once been one of the wonders of England, was reduced to just serving as a workhouse for the poorest of the poor.

A magazine in 1805 told how hundreds of people were crammed into rooms which had no proper toilets.

In short, it reeked.

Life was a little better for most working people - but only when the money was coming in.

In 1844-5 a Government report into big towns said about Norwich that there were up to ten people in a room, public sewers were poor - and everything stank in hot weather.

In 1848 another report estimated a fifth of the population was completely poor - so poor that they'd sold all their furniture to raise enough money just to live. They had hardly enough pennies to buy bread, let alone coal for the fire or even decent clothing. Children went barefoot. 'Neglect and decay are now conspicuous in the streets,' they said.

A year later reporters from the Morning Chronicle newspaper visited the city - and were shocked by what they found.

They told of lazy and greedy factory owners who did nothing for their workers. Children as young as 10 working long hours for just two shillings (10p) a week. No public washing facilities.

And terrible, terrible houses. Step this way while we go into two of them. Oh, and you'd better hold your nose...

House 1: 'Hello, I'm a gauze weaver. I live in a house in White Lion Court, St Paul's. There's no chance of any privacy because there's 12 houses in our court.

'There's also a stable - and a slaughterhouse. The noise and smell from the slaughterhouse is terrible! But what's worse is the privy next door... because it leaks! Imagine living in a house with poo coming through the walls. There's no chance of any fresh air, because I have to stay here and work from dawn to 11pm at night to try to make enough money for my four children.'

House 2: 'I'm a weaver too. I live in Light Horseman Yard. It sounds a nice address, doesn't it? But it's really cramped, with eight houses in it.

'My family live in three rooms - my married daughter lives in the bottom one and I live in the middle one with my wife and two children.

'The top one? That's for

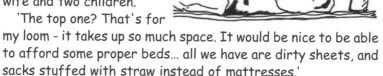

my loom - it takes up so much space. It would be nice to be able to afford some proper beds... all we have are dirty sheets, and sacks stuffed with straw instead of mattresses.'

Light Horseman Yard was in Pockthorpe, which was the area just over the Wensum by Bishop's Bridge. It was just about the nastiest place in Victorian Norwich. In the 1850s there were 35 pubs and 3300 people, just about all of them crammed into horrible homes. A visiting rector wrote in 1872 that this was 'a vile neighbourhood'.

The Lee Report

Soon after the newspaper stories, the Government sent in an inspector to examine the city.

William Lee toured the city over eight days and saw for himself how bad things were.

...churchyards so full of dead people that their bones were sticking out of the soil.

...the Wensum polluted by 138 different drains from sewers, toilets, slaughterhouses and factories.

... water 'bad in quantity, bad in quality and bad in everything that should constitute a water supply.'

The inquiry heard that more than 14,000 people were involved in weaving and families struggled to even afford one room to live in. As for fresh air and clean water, forget it.

As ever, it was the children who paid the heaviest price. In 1849, the inquiry heard, more than a third of the people who died the year before were aged five and under.

Water supply was truly shocking. Sometimes up to 50 families shared just *one* tap. There were only ten public pumps in the whole city - and some of those were next to those yucky churchyards.

The drains were even worse. The water in the creek from Mr Will's skin yard was described like this: 'the whole surface was boiling with foul gases, accompanied with constant hissing from the explosion of the bubbles.'

Fancy a dip? I thought not.

Lee described the foul ditch in Pockthorpe - which had no piped water, no drains and no lights - as 'one of the most horrible places I have ever seen'.

A local surgeon told the Lee inquiry that people who lived in houses built against the city walls often didn't even have privies. People living upstairs, if they were clean by nature, carried their 'excrementitious matters' [= poo!] to the nearest bin 'but in some cases they empty all sorts of abominations out of the window'. Watch out below!

Water shame

Mr Lee spoke again and again in his report about the need to get proper water supplies to people. Only a fifth of homes in 1849 had piped water (and even that was full of nasty insects and bugs).

The criticism worked. After a while anyway. In 1854 a new water company was set up - but that didn't solve problems for a long time (although a reasonable supply of water meant the city could set up its own fire service).

In 1854 another outbreak of cholera hit the city - described as 'very bad' by a local priest.

In 1859 the famous engineer Joseph Bazalgette (who had worked out how to improve London's terrible sewers, which made him just about the world's top expert on poo) told councillors they had to spend £80,000 on building two sewers urgently. But the council decided to spend just £10,000 instead.

Samuel Clarke wrote a series of letters to the Norfolk Chronicle from November 1863 which revealed to the posh folk of the city just how dreadful things still were. Because the weaving industry was in decline people were even poorer than they had been at the time of Lee's report. One family of five, he wrote, had only one straw bed between them. One child was paralysed, another blind.

But it was not until 1867 that the two sewers were built, and not until the 1890s that improved water supply and sewerage started to reduce the number of children dying from nasty diseases.

Boots to the rescue!

Wobbly weavers

As we've seen weaving had been making money for Norwich for centuries. But the storm clouds were gathering.

The cloth industry of Yorkshire and Lancashire had grown very quickly - with lots of big mills, the latest machines, cheap power and plenty of places where they could sell their cloth.

Norwich was still the top producer of the special worsted cloth. But thousands of weavers working in attics by hand couldn't compete with huge machines.

There were plenty of ups and downs to come...

DOWN... Britain's long war with France at the start of the century (The Napoleonic Wars) and its after-effects hit the weaving trade hard until the 1830s.

UP... Norwich firms started making a type of cloth called 'crepe' in 1822. This was dyed black and used by people who were in mourning for dead loved ones. And there were a lot of dead loved ones in South America and Mediterranean judging by the popularity of Norwich crepe.

But that year also saw wage cuts for Norwich workers – so they rioted. And in 1827. And 1829.

DOWN... Things got worse when The East India Company (which controlled trade to India) stopped sending Norwich camlets (a light cloth used for cloaks) east in 1833 - Norwich's place had been snatched by Yorkshire cloth makers.

UP... Steam-powered mills started in Norwich after 1834 which at last meant the city could start competing with Yorkshire, but if you still worked by hand then it was definitely a...

DOWN... because your wages slumped and you struggled to live in even the tiniest, smelliest court or yard. The Royal Commission on Textiles in 1839 visited Norwich and found 5073 hand-looms in the city - with 1021 weavers unemployed.

Faced with cuts in wages the weavers rioted – again – and went on strike.

UP... fashion came to the rescue in the middle years of the century, when finely-woven Norwich shawls became THE thing to have draped around your shoulders. Even Mrs Charles Dickens had one. Norwich hair-cloths, too, began to be fashionable in the 1850s.

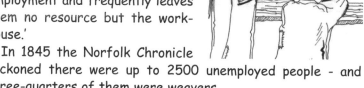

'The latest fashion is for sacking people'

But as Government inspector Lee pointed out in his 1850 report: 'A change in fashions will throw thousands of people out of employment and frequently leaves them no resource but the workhouse.'

In 1845 the Norfolk Chronicle reckoned there were up to 2500 unemployed people - and three-quarters of them were weavers.

By the 1860s the number of looms had declined to only a thousand or so. A new workhouse was built on Bowthorpe Road in 1859 because of the rising numbers of poor people - again, many of them weavers.

By the 1870s Yorkshire mills were able to do all the fine, high-value work that Norwich was famous for. And at the time of the 1891 Census there were only just over 1000 worsted weavers - and this in a city which now had almost 100,000 people in it.

Within a few years, even those jobs were gone. Weaving had ended up going definitely...

...**DOWN.**

Hooray for boots!

Norwich needed more industry - and it needed it fast. Fortunately the answer was to be found on the end of your legs!

Everyone needs shoes and boots - and unlike, say, Norwich shawls, it's not something you have worry about falling out of fashion. No-one likes bare feet!

The leather industry had been big in Norwich for centuries - right back to medieval times. After cattle were killed for beef, their hides were a valuable by-product.

People used leather for belts, buckets, saddles - and shoes of course.

Round about 1800 a John Smith kept a shop near the market place. He had the smart idea of stocking a range of boots in different sizes.

The boot and shoe industry began to grow, helped by a big supply of cheap labour and the large number of local tanneries (where the leather was prepared).

From the mid-19th century the industry grew quickly. In 1862 there were around 3000 people in the trade - within six years this had almost doubled.

By 1870 leather working had taken over from weaving as Norwich's main industry. And by 1900 there were 8000 people involved in making boots and shoes, or in preparation work. This was 16 times the number who had worked in the industry in 1800.

If weavers had a bit of reputation for having the occasional riot, then leather workers had the reputation for having the occasional pint of beer. Rather more than a pint, actually.

You see, leather workers were paid for 'piece work' - they got paid per bit of work they did, and not a wage. This meant they couldn't really have holidays - so they made the most of their weekends. By getting thoroughly drunk.

In fact they drunk so much over the weekend that they often ended up still drinking when Monday came around.

This unofficial holiday became known as 'St Monday' because of the old custom of having saints' days off as holidays. But the bad news for local pubs after 1860 was more and more people working in factories instead of from home.

Hot stuff!

Norwich became world-famous for something yellow.

No, not canaries (or even The Canaries) - but mustard.

Putting a splodge of the hot sauce on your dinner plate became hugely popular, and when Jeremiah Colman moved his works from Stoke Holy Cross to Carrow in the 1850s it was the signal for Norwich mustard to become world-famous.

It would be fitting in a book called Nasty Norwich to tell you what a rotten boss he was. Except it wouldn't be true.

The factory boss was, in fact, described as 'a merchant prince of the best type'. His Carrow works, which had grown to the size of 13 football pitches by the end of the century, were full of things to help his workers have nicer lives.

'Are you SURE that mustard's not too hot, dear?'

JJ Colman and his wife started the Carrow Social Welfare Scheme, which included a school (with 342 pupils by the time changes in 1870 set up the national schools system we have today).

He had a canteen where workers could have meat and vegetable stew and a pint of coffee for 4d (2p). The firm even had its own nurses for workers.

Velocipedes... and chopped-up worms

Let's end by saluting two Norwich inventors. The first was a Mr J Ayton, described as a man with a genius for invention.

129

Among his bright ideas were a 'returning jumper' (a thing for improving milling machinery, not something for taking a dodgy sweater back to the shop), an iron suspension wheel in 1826, and a double double bass (for really, really DEEP NOTES for musicians). One of his most interesting inventions was a 'velocipede' - a sort of bike - 'whereby with a few stones of luggage a person may travel with ease short journeys up to six miles an hour and longer journeys at about five.'

One person went 80 miles (about 130 km) in 18 hours on an Ayrton machine. History doesn't record just how sore his bum was when he'd finished!

And he even invented a sort of rollerblade (with two 15cm-diameter iron wheels on each foot) which let you travel up to 15km an hour. So why didn't they catch on? Perhaps it was the terrible name he thought up for them... 'tachypos'.

Our second clever-clogs was Charles Barnard. In 1844 he invented the first-ever wire-weaving machine for making fences.

Suddenly you didn't have to nail together fences - you could **KNIT** them! The whole world wanted Barnard's clever invention. By 1935, it was said that his fencing 'defends Australia from rabbits, South Africa from jackals, forms fox farms in Scandinavia and fences innumerable estates.'

He also had clever ideas about the heating of large buildings by hot water, and using iron and glass in building.

Charles also invented a noiseless lawnmower, which was bad news for hard-of-hearing worms who'd popped out of their holes out for a look.

It wasn't all work - let's see how people let their hair down.

Fun... and fighting

Having fun...
...in the 19th century depended on how rich you were. And, often, how much you'd had to drink too. Let's take a look at some of the ways you could relax in 19th-century Norwich.

Be nasty to animals
Two of the biggest 'sports' in Norwich were cock-fighting (a favourite, as we've already seen, in local pubs) and also bull-baiting, when a pack of dogs was set on a bull tied to a post. One contest in 1807 was said to have provided 'very great sport'. Not for the poor animals, though.

Buy a picture
As we've seen, Norwich is famous for many things. Here's another: Norwich is one of the few places in Britain to have a style of painting named after it.

John Sell Cotman (1782-1842) and John Crome (1768-1821) were famous landscape painters, two of the Norwich School's best-known members - and great rivals.

John Crome had a very good reason to keep painting - he and his wife had at least nine children. His landscapes are found in lots of posh museums these days, but at the time some people looked at them and said 'Er - I don't think you've *quite* finished that one, Mr Crome'.

'Er, better hurry up and paint some more, John... I've just been to the doctors...'

That meant he only got around 15 guineas (£15.75) for his pictures.

But the London artist J M W Turner, who was *much* more famous, earned 500 guineas for his.

Crome often had to work as a picture dealer, teacher and even a portrait cleaner for the city council to make ends meet.

Crome was a bit of a rebel when he was younger. When he was a youth he worked as a surgery errand boy - until the day he threw a skeleton at some medical students! He also liked to swap round the labels on medicines he was delivering, the little scamp.

Having struggled to sell pictures in his lifetime, people cashed in on his fame after his death - by copying his work.

J S Cotman painted some of the most lovely landscapes in British painting - like Mousehold Heath and The Marl Pit - but, like Crome, he spent his life struggling to sell his paintings.

Cotman, like many other painters of his day, couldn't resist jazzing things up a bit. Often his landscapes would have some homely peasant wandering into view or well-behaved animals (definitely no cowpats here).

Sometimes we can catch him out. When he painted the Cow Tower he decided to include a - you've guessed it - cow standing in one of the windows. Trouble was, he forgot that the window wasn't very big... making the cow, oh, about a metre and a bit tall!

Go to the theatre

Norwich had its own theatre as early as 1758 - the second oldest purpose-built theatre in England. It was rebuilt and renovated in 1801 - but soon faced a keen rival in the nearby White Swan Inn.

Each theatre tried to out-do the other for crowd-pleasing spectacle and performances were often the excuse for riots and rowdiness.

When the Theatre Royal was rebuilt (again) in 1826, its opening night was marred by 'vulgar blockheads' who attacked the person in the refreshment kiosk.

What could you see at these places? Famous circus performers like the tiny General Tom Thumb in 1844 and the daredevil tight-rope walker Blondin (he once walked over Niagara Falls). Or it could be waxworks or freak shows.

In 1828 Mr Ching Lau Lauro ('the celebrated posture master and buffo') performed at the theatre 'amid universal hisses which such trash called for – in spite of Lauro swallowing his own head'. Now *that's* what we call a trick...

'No madam, I'm NOT one of the waxworks – I'm the manager!'

The Theatre Royal asked the city magistrates to close down a rival, the Adelphi (or Ranelagh Gardens) because it was 'immoral to the highest degree'.

It closed in 1849 anyway, to make way for Norwich's Victoria rail station.

Pleasure gardens were found in several places in Norwich.

They were a sort of open-air theatre, circus and drinking club combined. You could play skittles, watch fireworks - or see people do pointless challenges, like John Mountjoy in 1840 who, in under an hour, ran a mile, walked backwards a mile, pushed a wheelbarrow a mile, trundled a hoop half a mile, hopped 220 yards and jumped over 30 hurdles. Oh, and picked up 40 hazelnuts from the floor with his mouth – and without letting his knees touch the ground once.

Try getting your teachers to let you do *that* on sports day!

From 1876 to 1882 the Vaudeville Theatre in St Giles (which started life as a roller-skating rink) offered everything from performing dogs to music hall.

Get drunk

They used to say about Norwich that it had a church for every week of the year and a pub for every day. But that was a severe under-estimate on the booze side.

In fact there were hundreds more - by the 1850s something like 650 licensed pubs and beer shops. There were 44 around the market place alone!

And 220 of those pubs were places where you could buy the company of a girlfriend as well as a pint.

As an idea of how much they drank, there used to be a group called the Everlasting Club which drank in the Maid's Head. You became a member if you drank so much that you couldn't sit on the wall of a nearby church without falling off!

The Victorians were very worried about what became known as 'The Drink Question'. In 1872 they tried to cut down the opening hours of pubs. So what did the drinkers do? Take big cans in with them to the pubs, fill them up just before closing time – and then sit out in the street and drink some more.

In 1879 the pages of the EDP were filled with letters from people concerned about there being one pub for every 130 people in Norwich (if those figures applied today there would be 930 pubs in the city!). They saw too many pubs as leading to poverty, crime and disease.

Hear a concert

While the poor people of Norwich sat in pubs having boozy sing-songs (when they weren't getting up to worse mischief), the posh class of Norwich wanted something a bit more genteel. And so the Norfolk and Norwich Triennial Festival was founded in 1824. 'Triennial' meant it was held every three years. There were two things you needed if you went to a concert in St Andrew's Hall: a tough bum and a good umbrella.

The tough bum came in handy because many of the concerts went on and on and on - often to midnight and after. And the umbrella? Well, sadly the roof of the hall was notorious for leaking. On one occasion a cello player had to do a recital with someone holding a brolly over him!

See a fight
One of the most popular activities in the early years of the century was prize-fighting. This wasn't like modern boxing with a few rounds and the fighters wearing gloves. This was two blokes standing in a field hitting each other with bare fists. Contests could go on for hours and hours - and boxers sometimes died as a result.

Writer George Borrow, the man who coined the phrase 'a fine city' for Norwich (actually he wrote 'a fine *old* city') told about one bruising encounter between the 'massive champion with a flattened nose', Tom Cribb, and a local boxer.

No prizes for guessing who won.

Go to the pictures
Yes, you could see a film in 19th-century Norwich. But only just. It was almost at the end of the century - 1896 - that the first moving pictures were shown locally at Agricultural Hall (now part of the Anglia Television site). There was no sound.

Well, only the noise of some dead-impressed city folk going 'oooh' and 'aaaah' at the sight of moving pictures.

Grow silly hairstyles
Ask your grandparents who first wore quiffs - a bit of hair either brushed up or smoothed down over the forehead - and I bet they'll say Teddy Boys, the rock and roll fans of the 1950s. And they'd be wrong!

For Norwich youths were there half a century earlier.

Here's what James Hooper had to say in 1899: 'I have never seen the word 'quiff' in print but it is used, at any rate in Norwich, to denote that tuft of hair worn by many Norwich youths, of the rougher sort, mostly projecting over their foreheads.

'They seem to consider that these hairy forelocks given them a rake-helly or devil-may-care aspect...'

Rock and roll might still be 50 years or more away, but the quiff boys of Norwich had plenty in common with the 'teds': they both thought they were the coolest teenagers around!

Tell a ghost story

Victorians *loved* ghost stories – and with all the dark old buildings in Norwich there were plenty to tell.

But they could frighten each other with other strange tales too – like the time (around 1858) when people swore they had seen a mysterious devil in a long black cloak suddenly appear from nowhere to frighten people in Chapelfield.

'That hideous figure's either Spring-Heeled Jack – or my Bert's fallen in the dung-heap again!'

So many people believed the story of 'Spring Heeled Jack' that crowds flocked to the area in the hope of catching a glimpse of the evil visitor!

Watch an execution

One of the most popular pastimes of the lot! No, really. Let's meet some of those who took part...

...willingly and unwillingly!

Cruel crimes and nasty justice

Dying to be a criminal

There was plenty of punishment around for those Norwich people who fell into bad ways.

The castle was still being used as a prison and it had been adapted for the county jail in 1792-3. As well as housing hundreds of people who were later transported to Australia, there were plenty whose journey was rather shorter.

Like Martha Alden, who murdered her husband while he was asleep. She was hanged at the castle in July 1807. Her execution was watched by a large crowd, which might seem like a cruel thing to do - but people did. In fact they absolutely *loved* it, and the more notorious the murderer the better. Great Yarmouth killer Samuel Yarham's demise at the castle in 1846 was watched by a reported 30,000 people - many of who ended up rioting and drunk.

So much for scaring them about crime.

And that was topped by the execution of double murderer James Blomfield Rush in 1849. People even came from London on the train on specially-arranged return tickets to watch the hanging.

'So I expect you won't be needing that return train ticket now...'

Slowly the mood for public hangings began to change. But the last public execution at the castle was as late as 1867. That was 22-year-old Hubbard Langley, who had killed his uncle.

Eyewitnesses told of huge crowds packing every inch of the cattle market (now the park over Castle Mall) and even the roofs of buildings. Here's how one account continued: 'Langley stood for a minute or two under the beam while the white cap was being drawn over his face, and the rope adjusted. Some church bell was tolling out while the clergyman read the burial service.

'Suddenly I heard a piercing scream and a woman fell insensible at my feet. Looking towards the scaffold I saw only a rope slowly swinging from side to side...'

To help you remember the executions you could buy a sheet with the 'true confessions' of the doomed criminal (made up and printed in advance). Or afterwards you could see the death-masks showing what the condemned prisoner looked like.

And you can still see some of these at the Castle Museum... if you dare!

Escape!

Not everyone who was imprisoned at the castle stayed put. People had been escaping on and off for years. Like the Lynn sailor called Galloway who ran away with his pal James Ayers in 1789 and went on a spree of thefts. He was caught and executed - which didn't stop others from trying to escape.

In 1837 Henry Pettel tore his blanket into strips and knotted them together.

But he fell off the top of the castle, a report of the time saying that 'he pitched his head into a bucket' and was - surprise, surprise - 'somewhat seriously injured'.

'You're looking a little pail...'

138

William Brooks was even unluckier in 1830. On trial for high-way robbery, he tried the old knotted blankets trick too.

And like Pettel seven years later, it broke. Brooks fell 70 feet - about 21 metres. He broke his thigh, pelvis, left arm and every one of the ribs on his left side, plus ended up with a horrible lump on the back of his head. He had to be carried into court on the back of a warder.

The court heard that Brooks was now a helpless cripple.

Guess what? He was sentenced to be transported anyway.

Criminals didn't like to stay in the old City Gaol (near the Guildhall) either. One of the most daring escapes was in 1808 when Mary Hudson managed to take the bricks out of a 60cm-thick wall, hide them under her bed, and squeeze out – with her six-month-old baby in tow.

The invasion of the body-snatchers

The yuckiest criminals? They had to be the body-snatchers, who were around in the early part of the century.

The problem was that medical students were always desperate for people to practise on. Dead people, that is.

And so the snatchers would hide around a corner when a funeral was on, then nip over the wall with a spade when no-one was looking.

One of the strangest cases came in 1838 when a vet, George Perowne, turned up at the house of the recently-dead John Maxey and pinched his body. When his widow complained, Perowne claimed that Maxey had promised him his body before he died.

Perowne was taken to court. And got off!

May the force be with you

Norwich got its first proper police force in 1836. It was just 18 men and a superintendent. This had grown to 80 by 1851 - but they had their hands full trying to control the citizens, as we'll soon see.

And talking of new things, we should mention the City of Norwich Gaol, which was built in 1827 (it's where the Roman Catholic cathedral now stands). Like the castle jail, it had a treadmill - a wooden wheel which inmates were forced to walk on for hour after hour, sometimes up to 12 hours a day.

Criminal? I feel more like a hamster!

The jail closed in 1881 - and the castle, after hundreds of years as a prison, was soon to follow. It shut in 1887 and was sold by the Government to be turned into the famous Castle Museum.

Fire! Fire!

Another modern thing Norwich got in the 19th century was a city fire service. Up to the 1850s most of the fire-fighting was done by firemen paid for by big insurance companies, like Norwich Union.

The city had a couple of its own fire engines, and fires often ended up with private firemen, city firemen, police and any passing soldiers all turning up at once. It was chaos!

A typical example was what happened in 1811 when a warehouse near the market place caught fire. A newspaper report said: 'fire engines were inefficient, and the appliances out of repair'. Not even a troop of soldiers could stop the blaze.

So in 1858 a proper city fire service was formed.

Not that they didn't have a few teething problems.

They used to alert the crews that there was a fire by sending a big rocket into the sky.

Until the day in 1876 when one ended up going through an open window at a printing firm, and, er, setting fire to it!

Oops!

Sick of Norwich

The new plagues

That 1844-5 Government report about Norwich slums had this conclusion: 'It is here that epidemics make their earliest seizure, that they remain the longest and that prove to be the most severe.'

Chilling words - and true.

Poverty and rotten housing was linked with nasty diseases as sure as night follows day.

Lee's 1850 report spoke of outbreaks of measles, scarlet fever, cholera, erysipelas (no, I can't pronounce it either, but it is basically a disease causing large red patches on the skin) and horrible eye infections.

But looking back to earlier in the century things weren't any better.

There were smallpox outbreaks in 1812, 1813, 1819 and 1839, costing hundreds of lives - and nearly all of them were children.

Perhaps the biggest single killer over the century was tuberculosis, known as TB, a disease of the lungs known as 'consumption' in Victorian times.

Its symptoms included fever, weight loss and spitting of blood, and was made worse by poor diet.

Cholera, a terrible disease which produces acute vomiting and diarrhoea (non-stop pooing), arrived in Britain in 1831 - and just a year later it was claiming lives in Norwich.

Official figures say 128 died between August and October.

The people were urged to stop boozing, stop eating heavy suppers (cut out those Norfolk dumplings) and even not to get cross.

And just like all those orders which had been made at the time of Tudor plagues, it proved pretty useless advice.

Cholera returned again and again.

It didn't help that there were some very strange ideas going round. Like the case recorded in April 1840 of sick children being taken to a certain woman in St Margaret's parish to be treated for 'spinnage'.

This involved having the lobes of their right ears cut (for 3d - nearly 2p) and the sign of the Cross made in the blood on the forehead and breast of the child. And the same thing to the left ear the following week. And again. And again. Up to NINE times.

But it didn't cure spinnage. Why? Because there was *no such disease*.

Lee's 1850 report listed examples of dirty houses, crowded courts and yucky yards leading to diseases galore.

The list makes grim reading, but one in particular stands out. This was the yard in St Swithin's parish where the 1849 outbreak of cholera began. A total of nine people died there.

And the name of this place?

Coffin Yard...

Kicking up a stink

The pongy, dirty conditions produced more victims.

Like another smallpox outbreak in 1872, killing up to 30 people per week.

The first medical officer of health for the city reported in 1873 that a quarter of the deaths recorded were of children aged under five - a figure scarcely better than the 1849 figure. He blamed bad diet and bad housing, and use of drugs like opium. He said this was due to 'much ignorance among the poorer classes as to the proper way of bringing up infants'.

A rise in scarlet fever cases from 1873 to 1878 was blamed on the introduction of schools for all children. As everyone was supposed to go to school (they still are - bad luck) it forced teachers to keep sick pupils in class. Typhus and scarlet fever broke out again around 1880.

You would have thought the powers-that-be would take the hint. But as late as 1893 there were still 20,000 homes without a proper flushing toilet. They used primitive loos called privies - or just chucked things on a pile. The city council did collect the contents every Friday - but the loos never got clean.

As late as the 1920s the privy or 'petty' was known in Norwich as 'the chocolate box' (you can guess why!) and the lucky people who had to collect its contents were known as 'violet men', presumably because sweet-smelling violets were the very last thing they smelt of!

'A box of chocolates for me? How nice!'

The century ended as it began - with disease.

A typhoid outbreak in 1898 cost 98 lives, a grim reminder that the war against disease was one that still had to be won.

As for the horrible slum houses, efforts to knock them down didn't really get going until the 1870s - but it was a slow and expensive job which took until well into the 20th century. By 1900 there were still more than 700 of the stinky 'courts' of pre-1860 houses.

A 'Fine City'? Not if you lived in those places.

Hospital havoc

Meanwhile, things were changing at the Norfolk and Norwich Hospital.

In 1847 surgical patients at the N&N were able to use the new wonder chemical chloroform for the first time.

This freed them from pain while the operations were being carried out. By the following year, the medical staff were able to tell the hospital governors the experiment was a complete success. In reply the governors asked if the surgeons could now do something about 'stopping sound from the operation room'. Clearly, some patients hadn't quite stopped screaming *just* yet.

After all the sickness of the early 19th century, things began to improve by the 1870s. Smallpox and typhus were beginning to go, at last.

So everything in the garden was rosy? Not quite.

The N and N bosses may have thought they were being smart in using the latest Lister carbolic spraying machine for killing germs in the air.

And they were. The trouble was, no-one had realised that you had to wash your hands and surgical instruments too.

Everyone dreaded surgery - because you stood a one in 14 chance of dying from an operation. In fact the death rates in the 1870s were no better than the 1840s.

Then there were the perils of being on the wards. Despite efforts to be clean and tidy, there were still cases of patients contracting diseases such as smallpox (1861), pyaemia (blood poisoning) and erysipelas (1874-5).

On one tragic occasion in 1875 the killer was in human and not microscopic shape. A mentally-ill patient, Robert Edwards, ran amok with a pair of tongs and murdered three children.

But things were getting better for patients. In 1877 the governors were told of big improvements in the surgery death rates... and the hospital's toilets.

And from 1879-1883 the Norfolk and Norwich Hospital was almost rebuilt and made much more modern. In 1887 the hospital was able to drop its century-old rule that so-called 'incurable' patients couldn't be admitted for treatment.

And two years later the nurses had their own special cause for celebration: hot water in their dormitories!

On and off the rails

Far, far away

Amazing but true: A message could travel from Norwich to London in just 17 *minutes* from 1808 using the military telegraph system (yes really, but they closed it down in 1815 when we finally beat Napoleon).

But messages were one thing, people were another.

Norwich was still a long way from anywhere in 1800. You could take a coach to London and you *might* get there in a day - but it would be a long and uncomfortable journey over rotten roads.

Or you could take a wherry boat to Great Yarmouth, hoping to sail on from there. But if the wherry was full of goods it could take 16 hours just to get to the coast.

They tried to get a steamship service going in the early years of the century. But a boiler explosion killed eight adults (another died later in hospital) and drowned a child - and that was the end of that. By the late 1820s you could take a paddle steamer from Norwich to London, but it still took 17 hours (and landowners

'Great. Now all they have to do is invent the railways!'

didn't like the way it damaged the river banks).

Ah ha, thought someone. What if we dig a 'new cut' so boats can take a short cut to the Waveney (and then to Lowestoft)? Wouldn't that help? The plan was agreed in 1827 and passed in 1833... but it just didn't work. The company behind it struggled on for a few more years and then closed.

What was needed was for someone to hurry up and invent the railway. And in 1825, somebody did. Well, nearly.

Railway rivals

The great idea was this: why don't we build a 'Norfolk and Suffolk Railway'? The idea was that Norwich weavers could take their stuff down to London and make pots of money. But the enormous cost - close to a million pounds - put off many investors. And then there was a scandal over what happened to the money they did raise. So the whole thing collapsed.

Flop number 1.

In 1836 a law was passed for an Eastern Counties railway from London to Norwich. But it took until 1843 just to get to Colchester. And then stopped! Flop number 2.

But at least the railway line from Norwich to Yarmouth had been built by now. When it opened in 1844 more than a thousand people crammed aboard for the opening trip. Suddenly the journey to Yarmouth had shrunk from several hours to just 50 minutes.

A year later the first train travelled from Norwich to London (Shoreditch). It had to go via Cambridge rather than Ipswich but was still hours quicker than the coach (four hours twenty minutes v 13 hours).

In the mid-1840s you could choose from up to seven daily services by coach and horses to London.

But within seven months of that first rail trip, all were gone.

The coach age had given way to the rail age.

Slow, slow….

Those early rail journeys were certainly eventful. Here's the story of one young lady who tried to travel from Yarmouth to London, via Norwich, on February 1 1846.

She set out from Yarmouth at 2.30pm. Then the train left the rails at Norwich. Delay.

A huge wait at Ely with no explanation. More delay.

Another ten-minute wait at Cambridge….

The train took so long that people in London were terrified that it had crashed - there had been several accidents in the line's history already and there was no way of finding out, because telegraph links between stations didn't come in until around 1847. It's amazing there weren't more crashes, if you think about it.

Anyway, our poor young lady eventually got into London at 4am - *13 and a half hours* after setting off!

A second Norwich railway station - Victoria - was opened in 1849 for the London-Ipswich-Norwich trains, but it soon became clear it wasn't really needed. But it only closed to passenger trains in 1916.

And a third - City Station - followed in 1882 (it closed in 1969).

The railways were so power-ful by now that it was seriously suggested in 1881 that the line should end up at the cattle market (now the park by the Castle)... by going across Cathedral Close and smashing down the beautiful Erpingham

Gate. The cathedral staff had to appeal all the way to Parliament before the crazy idea was stopped.

The Thorpe Disaster

There were several accidents and near-disasters on the new railways. Like in July 1865 when the London-Norwich express came off the rails near the river Yare and stopped – just – on the bridge. No-one was hurt.

But on September 11 1874, disaster finally struck.

Two trains collided at Thorpe, killing both drivers and firemen and 21 passengers. Sixty more were left injured.

What had happened was staff at Brundall had let the train from Great Yarmouth through when the line wasn't clear. They'd realised their mistake immediately, but could only wait helplessly for the terrible accident to happen.

The 8.40pm from Yarmouth and Lowestoft hit a 14-carriage express 'with a noise like thunder'. The night inspector who should have spotted the mistake was jailed for eight months for manslaughter.

All change!

Despite setbacks like these, the railways changed things for ever. In all sorts of ways too. Now you could go to Yarmouth or Cambridge on a day-trip - or even London.

The Yarmouth line even held the national speed record at one time - a train covering a mile (1.6 kilometres) in just 44 seconds.

The railways brought new types of fresh food to Norwich. Thousands of people passed through Norwich on their way to holidays on the coast. And loads of new jobs were created for drivers, clerks, porters, tracklayers...

The success of the railways also spelled the end for a plan to build a new harbour in Norwich (that's why there used to be a pub called the 'Clarence Harbour' near the football ground).

Even *time* had to change!

Before the railways, every town in Britain worked to a slightly different time. Norwich was actually three minutes ahead of London. But when the trains started, the time needed to be the same across the country for the new timetables to work - so Norwich lost its 180-second lead on the capital.

And even the *riots* weren't quite the same any more. In 1851 the authorities got wind of some Great Yarmouth seamen about to start trouble. The police and soldiers grabbed a train at Norwich - and jumped off in Yarmouth just 50 minutes later to stop them!

Vote for Me!

The rotten city

Norwich was famous for its cloth... and its rotten politicians.

Only a few people had the vote - and some were quite happy to sell their favours to the highest bidder. It was even said local brewers had a special strong beer made for bribing voters.

Many people thought more people should have the vote. But those who were in power said 'NO!' (surprise, surprise).

Then there were big political issues like the Corn Laws (which kept the cost of bread high). In 1825 Lord Albermarle was only rescued from a mob outside the Angel pub (where Royal Arcade is now) by a passing butcher who let loose a bull to take their mind off attacking him.

There must have been something about that pub, for in 1830 supporters of the two political parties the Whigs and the Tories started a huge fight outside which quickly spread to the Castle Hill. Troops had to be called in to stop them.

Earlier in 1820 there were serious riots over the way the future king George IV had treated his wife Caroline of Brunswick.

But it was the bribery which was the worst thing.

Norwich became famous for its buying and selling of votes.

In 1827 Lieutenant White – who had just been beaten in a city election – said: 'I consider my failure more honourable than to have gained the day by bribery and corruption.'

No sour grapes there, then.

And Edward Taylor wrote in 1833 how it was 'dragged into infamous notoriety by its corrupt electors'.

Lots of newspapers started up in Norwich in the 1800s, mainly to support one political side or another, like the Norfolk News started in 1844 by reformer Jacob Henry Tillett, and the Eastern Counties Daily Press (now the EDP) by Jeremiah James Colman and Thomas Jarrold in 1870.

Thousands of people supported a movement called Chartism in the 1830s and 1840s to try to get a fairer system of voting.

Norwich had two great Chartist leaders: John Love, a weaver who attacked the cruel policy of splitting up married couples in workhouses (sadly, in a cruel twist of fate, he ended up in a workhouse himself).

The other was John Dover, who spent much of his time either trying to stir up the mob - or sometimes running from them (like the time he was accused of bribery).

He ended up being transported to Australia in 1845 for receiving stolen goods.

Even when the voting system was changed, bribery was still a problem. There was a big bribery scandal in 1859, and a would-be MP was exposed as a card cheat in 1865. In 1869 Sir Henry Stracey was barred for buying votes in Pockthorpe. Two years later Radical MP Jacob Henry Tillett was unseated for bribery too (and again in 1875). As late as 1885 Tory MP Harry Bullard was thrown out too.

Politics dull? Not in Norwich!

Making light of Norwich
Most of Norwich was dark and smelly.

But after about 1830 the posh people could have gas lighting - if they could afford it. This gas wasn't pumped from under the North Sea like the gas in your home today. It was made from coal instead. Extracting it was a dirty, smoky job.

When they wanted to build a new gasworks in Norwich in 1858 where do you think they built it?

On one of those empty fields around Norwich - or in one of the most historic parts of the city?

Yes, you've guessed it.

The gasworks at St Martin at Palace Plain meant fumes, smoke and dirt ended up blowing over the cathedral and city centre houses.

And putting it there also destroyed or damaged several precious old buildings, including the townhouse of Sir Thomas Erpingham, one of Henry V's most famous knights at the battle of Agincourt in 1421 (the Brits beat the French).

Did the builders learn from their mistake? No - in 1880 they made the gasworks even bigger.

The big clean-up

From the 1850s the city authorities tried to put right all the wrongs of the past centuries. As we've seen, they tried to build sewers, have cleaner streets, bring better water, knock down slum houses and lots of other things.

They quickly realised this was going to be a BIG, BIG job. Luckily in 1889 a law was passed called the Norwich Corporation Act which gave the city council the power to go and borrow lots of money to help get the job done. Just as well, really, because the city's population crashed through the 100,000 barrier by 1891.

So would they succeed? Let's step into the 20th century and find out.

Oh, and bring your steel helmet. It's going to get nasty there too!

The Terrible Twentieth Century

New century, new problems

A new century also meant a new census in 1901 - and with 111,000 people, Norwich had grown by a tenth in just a decade. So where were all these people living?

Well, in many cases out in suburbs like Catton and Sprowston (which had been swallowed up by Norwich City Council in 1888). Since 1877 there had been a big increase in terraced houses out in what is now called the 'Golden Triangle'.

But many - too many - still lived in the terrible slums in the old city. In 1900 there were still more than 700 of the old-style courts and yards tucked away behind the city streets.

Each court had up to 40 families living in awful conditions. Some were even below the level of the street and were known as 'holes'. Being lower than the street meant that all the rubbish, horse poo and other unmentionables were washed into the yards whenever it rained, making a smelly, dirty place even worse.

They were dark and dank places.

One, Jenkin's Alley off Oak Street, was so narrow it was nicknamed 'Chafe Lug' (= 'Scrape Ear').

What was life like for the people in these yards? Photographs from the time show barefoot children walking round in the dirt, with perhaps a few chickens rooting around for scraps (and adding their own poo to the mess, of course). The writer Eric Fowler remembered the yards from the 1930s when the mothers were 'old at 30' and left 'ugly and toothless' by the conditions.

Talking of toothless, a 1909 survey reckon more than eight in ten Norwich children had bad teeth. The working classes didn't do anything about their teeth until they were so rotten they had to be extracted.

Many people saw natural teeth as a nuisance and couldn't wait to have them pulled out. The good old days? What do *you* think?

A 1910 social survey of Norwich talked of the 'relatively high' incidence of TB in the city. A year earlier there had been an outbreak of typhoid fever caused by some dodgy shellfish.

The city authorities were trying their best. A third of the yards were improved in the first ten years of the century.

But of the 749 courts and yards still left by 1910, there were 'to be found housing conditions as bad and insanitary as those found anywhere'.

This left its mark on the people who lived there. That 1910 survey looked at the heights and weights of poor people and 'the better class'.

Poorer boys and girls aged three were, on average, five cm shorter than their richer counterparts.

Aged 13, the difference between rich and poor was even more marked. Poor boys weighed around 35kg - 2.8kg below the national average. It was even worse for the girls - they were 5.5kg below the national average - and still up to 5cm shorter (144cm v 149cm) than the richer kids.

The city council tried to sort out the slums by building Mile Cross from 1918-23, a council estate which was one of the first of its kind.

And after 1924 slum clearance was helped by the Government agreeing to cough up more cash. The 5000th slum clearance house was built by 1935.

But there was one casualty of all this improvement - Norwich's history.

Something old, something new

Think about Elm Hill. Beautiful isn't it? All those lovely old houses and that pretty cobbled street. No wonder tens of thousands of visitors enjoy walking up and down it and taking zillions of pictures every year.

Now think about Westlegate. Not very exciting is it?

But Westlegate used to be just like Elm Hill: narrow and old and interesting. And there were *loads* of streets in Norwich like that.

So where are they now?

Splattered!

Why? Well there were lots of reasons. Here's a few: German bombs (see the chapter after next), slum clearance, traffic improvements - and trams.

Trams are a sort of cross between buses and trains. They were once common in just about every major town and city in Britain - and are one of the main reasons why loads of people started to live in the suburbs. For the first time you could live outside the city and travel to work easily.

Making room for the trams meant old buildings came down in roads like St Andrew's Street. Trams began in 1900 and were an instant hit (26,000 people rode on them on the very first day), running until 1935 - but buses and cars soon became even more popular.

They needed room to be made for them. So yet more buildings came down. Even Norwich Castle mound had to be dug into to make space for them (the original road was about half the width it is today).

There were some people who tried to stick up for Norwich's heritage. The Norwich Society was born in 1923 when the city council had the idea of tearing down the last medieval bridge in the city (Bishopbridge - the very same one Robert Kett had marched over with his rebels in 1549). Elm Hill itself was saved from destruction by just *one* vote.

In 1911 the city council narrowly decided not to demolish the Guildhall. And just before the second world war someone said 'I know, let's knock down the Assembly House!'

Seems crazy now, doesn't it? But you have to remember that to a lot of people old houses meant grinding poverty and slums.

Getting rid of them would help Norwich the 'fine city' become the 'fine *modern* city'. And so they came down. Tudor houses, Stuart houses, medieval houses.

Splat.

Not everyone liked what they put up to replace them. Many houses and shops in Bethel Street and St Giles came down in the 1930s to make way for City Hall. It's now definitely one of Norwich's best-known buildings but one writer spoke of its 'stark ugliness' and to city folk at the time it was called 'the marmalade factory' because of the colour of the bricks.

Here's one incident which sums up the whole thing.

In 1936 the city council wanted to pull down 107 Pottergate to make way for an important new road.

Some people said it should be saved because it was one of the oldest houses in the city - but the Town Clerk sighed that Norwich was 'littered with old buildings'. Result: The house was flattened.

And the important new road? It was *never* built!

Foul Floods and Woeful War

Floods of tears

The river was always a mixed blessing for Norwich. It brought fresh water and trade - and was a way of travelling to Great Yarmouth and beyond. It was also, of course, full of poo and pollution.

But it usually behaved itself and stayed between its banks.

Every now and then, though, it flooded, filling the streets with even more poo and gungey mud. They were big floods, for instance, in 1614 and 1878.

There was a tradition that the old bridge of St Miles had a dragon's mouth carved in the middle. People used to say 'when the dragon drinks, Heigham sinks' - in other words, when the level got to the top of the bridge, the village (which was then right on the outskirts of Norwich) got flooded.

The dragon certainly would have had a lot to drink in 1912.

On August 26 of that year it started raining. Not the gentle shall-I-put-on-my-coat?-no-I'll-look-like-a-wuss kind but the heavy sort. The *really* heavy sort.

It rained and rained and rained non-stop for 29 hours. More than 18.5cm of it. By the middle of the next day the river began to flood. At Carrow Bridge it was an amazing 2.38m above low water level.

Upwards of 3500 homes were flooded for three days.

More than 40 houses were so damaged they had to be condemned.

Three people died: one woman from shock, a rescuer who slipped and drowned - and a baby who fell in the swirling waters while its mother was being saved. Many families lost everything - even their clothing - and all the city centre lights failed for three days. Just imagine what dark, horrible and damp nights they were for thousands of people.

There was a national appeal for the victims, with donations coming from as far away as South Africa.

After the flood the decision was taken to widen the river by four metres - back to where it was in Anglo-Saxon times.

War clouds

At the end of the 19th century no-one thought Norfolk was under any serious threat of invasion. The War Office suggested the best defence against raiders would be to have a special group of troops in Norwich... on bikes!

But the First World War changed Norwich, as it did every single town and village

'So that's sorted then: if the enemy invade - we let down their tyres!'

in Britain. When war broke out with Germany in August 1914 most people thought it would be over by Christmas.

It wasn't. It dragged on and on, and thousands of local soldiers died in the stinking trenches of France and Belgium.

Like the many men from Norwich who joined the Norfolk Regiment. A battalion raised in the city in 1914 lost 696 men in just two parts of just *one* battle on the Somme.

One Norwich parish - St Barnabas - suffered the greatest number of deaths of any parish in Norfolk. More than 170 of its menfolk were killed in action.

Back on the home front things were tough, with shortages of food and basic necessities. Factories in the city were turned over to war work - many jobs being taken by women. The engineering firm Boulton and Paul made 8645km of wire netting during the war - enough to stretch from Norwich to Brazil!

The firm also built more than 2000 aircraft and almost 8000 propellers. Mann Egerton made seaplanes from 1915, with both firms testing their new planes on an airfield built at Mousehold. Trying out the planes was dangerous work and there were many crashes - some fatal.

Other companies made boots for the soldiers and air corps.

The Norfolk and Norwich Hospital set aside 150 beds at the start of the war to treat the war wounded.

In the end 45,000 wounded troops were treated at Norwich War Hospital, established at the county asylum.

In January 1915 new horrors were added to war when two huge German airships called Zeppelins flew over the county.

Blown off-course (they thought they were attacking Hull in Yorkshire) one flew close to Norwich - but it was King's Lynn and Great Yarmouth which suffered bomb attacks. It can only have been luck that the city escaped.

In April 1916 city folk could hear the booming of the guns as German ships bombarded Lowestoft. It was a reminder of how close the war could be.

By the time the world's guns fell silent on November 11 1918, the cost of war was brought home to almost every family in Norwich and Norfolk.

The war had claimed the life of one man out of every nine in the county aged between 18 and 41. And that's not counting the thousands more left injured physically and mentally by the horrors. They would be 'fighting the war' for many more years to come.

In May 1919 there was another reminder of the horror. The body of the Norfolk nurse Edith Cavell was brought to rest at Norwich Cathedral from Belgium. She had been shot in 1915 by the Germans for helping Allied troops escape.

As the war ended thousands of troops came home, hoping to find that their sacrifice had created a better world.

They were soon to be disappointed.

Work and Play

When the guns fell silent...

...the surviving men from Norwich returned home from the trenches.

The first thing they said to the women who were working in their place was: 'Hey! Give us our jobs back!' (which the bosses did). The second thing was: 'Give us some more money!' (which the bosses didn't).

By late December 1918 there were riots and strikes for more pay. Jobless rates soared, and the response of many factory owners was to cut wages and increase workers' hours. One march later led to a riot in which a city store was broken into and looted by the hungry marchers.

What had gone wrong?

The war, of course. It held back much of Norwich's firms from making things to sell because of the need to switch to build warplanes and the like. And for those firms that weren't on war work, there was the problem of getting the raw materials to make things.

For Norwich's main industry - boots and shoes - there was another problem. In the first years of the century city firms employed around 10,000 people, with modern factories and many of the products going overseas to other countries. But the war meant the local firms couldn't sell abroad.

So other countries - like the United States - modernised *their* factories and pinched Norwich's trade.

If that seems familiar, it's because a very similar thing happened to the weaving trade in the early years of the century before. Then it had been black mourning cloth that had helped save local jobs. Now it was because everyone wanted to dance!

Norwich-made ladies' evening shoes, you see, were even better than those from oh-so-smart Vienna and Paris. That helped ease the post-war pain a bit.

The city council tried to make things better by building lots of new council houses, which as well as providing jobs also - as we've seen - helped get rid of horrible yards and courts. Jobless men were also set to work creating Norwich parks. Wensum Park (1924) and Waterloo Park (1931-3) were both made like this.

So at least some good things came out of all the nasty unemployment.

Work and pay
But let's step back in time (no pun intended!) a few years. That 1910 survey of the city tells us what people earned. For making shoes women were paid an average of three shillings (15p) a week - but the men were paid *four* times as much!

There were still a few people involved in weaving (about 700 at the start of the century) but that number was shrinking all the time.

In fact the number of weavers was dwarfed by the number of servants - three times as many (one of them was my nan).

Everyone worked hard. Railway carters usually worked from 6.30am to 7pm. Clothing workers went in from 8am to 7pm... that's 56 hours per week (Most people are supposed to work about 35-37 hours these days).

Another problem was that many jobs were very poorly paid. One worker even said: 'Once a man finds himself in Norwich he cannot easily get out of it.'

With a train ticket out of the city costing up to ten shillings (50p), it was very hard to save up enough.

It didn't help that spending money on boozing was still a major problem.

One notorious group was the drovers on the cattle market. The 'bullock-whackers', as they were known, did just that, hitting the poor beasts so they would go into the pens to be sold. They were often given a few coins by the grateful buyers... and went straight out and spent it on beer.

And as Norwich cattle market was the most important in England there was plenty of beer to be drunk.

One man who used to live in the yards wrote down his memories and told how many of the women had black eyes. Unfortunately violence towards women was the other price of a pint.

Norwich and the airship disaster

Boulton and Paul, you'll remember, became very good at making aircraft in the first world war.

So good, in fact, that they carried on making aircraft after the war ended.

But as well as making planes they also made the cleverly-designed steel frame which held together Britain's famous R101 airship.

The airships were giant cigar-shaped balloons fill with lighter-than-air gas. The trouble was that the gas they used - hydrogen - was incredibly dangerous. One tiny spark could make the whole thing explode.

And on one horrible day in autumn 1930 that's exactly what happened to the R101. Britain's airship industry died along with the blast - and Boulton and Paul's engineering genius was all for nothing.

Having fun

The 1910 survey said that 'The average under-educated factory operative who has been cramped for six days at one mechanical operation demands the wildest and most thrilling adventures by way of compensation.'

So what were these 'thrilling adventures'?

Apart from getting hideously drunk, you could see the newly-formed Norwich City Football Club for 3d (1.5p). From amateur beginnings in 1902 (it was founded by two teachers so, there, teachers aren't *so* bad are they?*), the team quickly became the biggest in the county.

In 1908 it moved to an old chalk pit off Rosary Road called The Nest. Thousands used to cram into it to see games - until a 1935 cup tie saw 25,000 squeeze in. Too many, said the safety inspectors. And so Carrow Road stadium was born.

Norwich City aren't called the Canaries for nothing! There were around 2-3000 canary breeders in the city who exported more than 30,000 birds from Norwich a year before the first world war.

*(*Stop pulling a face!)*

A game called logats was once very popular in Norwich. Did you play by...

A ...throwing horse poo at each other to see who could end up the smelliest?

B ...chucking big sticks at another stick?

C ...covering yourself with flour and pretending to be a ghost? (Answer: B)

Or you could go to the music hall. The Hippodrome opened on St Giles' Hill in 1903 (it was splattered by developers in 1960) and quickly became a firm favourite, as did the Victoria Hall in St Stephen's. A couple of pennies bought you a space on a bum-numbing wooden seat for an evening of music, song and novelty acts. The hall was supposed to seat 400, but sometimes 600 squeezed in!

Or you could go to see a film at the 'cinematograph'. Two pennies (about 1p in modern money) bought you a seat at a silent film show, where a pianist would play some suitable music when the exciting or sad bits came on.

Then, as now, the Theatre Royal was one of the most popular venues in the city.

But disaster struck in 1934 when it caught fire, which not only wrecked the building but destroyed most of its historic records at the same time. The theatre was rebuilt a year later.

But only a few years later such destruction was made to look small compared with what was just round the corner.

'Putting on that play about The Great Fire of London was asking for trouble!'

It was Norwich's worst disaster since the plague - and possibly the worst in its history.

We've saved the nastiest until last: The Second World War.

Woeful War - part 2

The dark clouds gather

The First World War was supposed to be 'the war to end all wars'. But by the early 1930s it was clear that the world was due for another batch of mayhem.

A power-mad party called the Nazis, led by Adolf Hitler, gained control of Germany and started to re-arm it... and soon set out to invade other countries.

For a while the politicians tried to talk their way out of trouble. But by 1938 it was a question of *when* war started up again, not *if*.

Norwich folk tried to get ready, by distributing gas masks in case there were poison gas attacks. Air raid shelters were dug. Trenches, too, were created in such places as Chapelfield Gardens.

Fateful September

The Germans invaded Poland in August 1939. It was one land grab too many. Britain told the Nazis to get out of Poland. They wouldn't.

So at 11am on Sunday September 3, Prime Minister Neville Chamberlain sadly told the country in a radio broadcast: 'this country is at war with Germany'.

That very afternoon the back gardens of Norwich were full of families digging holes for air-raid shelters, or rifling through sheds to find pieces of wood to protect their windows from shattering.

The dreaded air raid siren sounded at 2.42am the following morning. Everyone rushed out of their beds and into their shelters. Thirty-seven minutes later, the all-clear alarm was sounded.

It was first of many, many disturbed nights for the folk of Norwich.

The Phoney War

For the first few months of the war nothing really happened on home front, a period known as 'the Phoney War'. The feared bombing attacks didn't take place. The sirens kept going off and gradually people started to ignore them.

Not that people weren't beginning to suffer in other ways. In January 1940, rationing was introduced. You had to have special coupons to get bacon, butter and sugar with the idea of fair shares for all. Later, the scheme was extended to just about all food, drink, petrol and clothes.

Hotting up

In May 1940 the war suddenly got very serious very quickly. The Germans launched huge attacks on Belgium and Holland - and then headed for France.

That was also the month that the Local Defence Volunteers (the Home Guard) were formed - 30,000 men signed up in Norfolk by the end of the month alone.

The Home Guard were meant to help stop a German invasion if it came.

The Government also had secret plans - by 1941 there were 40 secret underground bases for 200 specially-trained troops who would attack any invaders. One of these secret hideouts was under Earlham golf course!

The terror begins

Norwich people were still not taking much notice of the air raid warnings.

Bernard Story, Norwich's head of air raid precautions warned: 'A sense of unreality still appears to exist... other people are being bombed, not us. All of us are apt to get slack and careless about air raid protection. Don't.'

People still didn't listen.

But after July 9 1940, they definitely did.

Around 5pm on that day, when many city workers were heading home, two German bombers suddenly appeared and dropped bombs on Barnard's factory on Mousehold (killing two people), Boulton and Paul (another ten dead, nearly 70 injured) and - worst of all - near Colman's, killing 15 workers on Carrow Hill.

People were angry that there had been no air raid warning. They would have been even angrier if they had heard the results of a secret inquiry which discovered that the bombers had been spotted *an hour* before they appeared over Norwich - and no-one had done anything to try and stop them.

It was a horrible lesson to everyone in the city that Norwich was one of the closest cities to occupied Europe, and easy to reach from Nazi airfields. But the worst was yet to come.

Danger UXB!

The nightmares didn't end when the raiders had dropped their cargoes of bombs and started heading back for Nazi-controlled Europe.

Sometimes the bombs didn't go off, but buried themselves deep into the street. The slightest jolt or movement could set them off hours, days, even months or years later. They were known as UXBs - unexploded bombs.

So they couldn't be left alone - someone had to try and take the fuses out of the bombs so they wouldn't explode. Not surprisingly, this was incredibly dangerous work.

Walk along Theatre Street and stand alongside the wall by St Stephen's Church. Looks pretty solid doesn't it?

But the only reason the church is still there is because of the bravery of a bomb disposal crew in September 1940. A huge 250kg bomb crashed through the pavement but didn't go off.

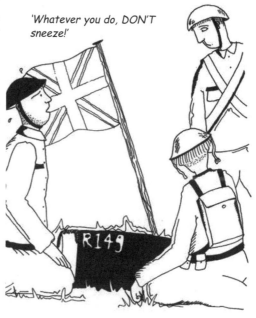

'Whatever you do, DON'T sneeze!'

A large area of the city centre was evacuated while the crew defused the bomb.

It took days to make it safe. And at any time it could have gone off - and that would have spelled instant death for the crew. But they stayed and did the job.

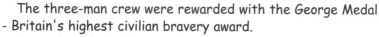

Could *you* have been that brave?

The three-man crew were rewarded with the George Medal - Britain's highest civilian bravery award.

Norwich Cathedral was the site of another alert in the same month. There were reports a bomb had fallen within yards of the building.

By an amazing chance the very spot it hit was an old well - so instead of exploding it just went straight down into soggy mud.

The Eastern Evening News of September 27 said a crew had dug down eight metres but found no trace. The authorities claimed people must have been mistaken.

But the bomb is thought to be still there to this day.

Rotten raids

Here's the story of just one small raid in February 1941.

It happened in Plumstead Road. A single German plane flew over and dropped around 20 bombs.

One man was just putting on his protective tin hat, ready to go outside to help, when there was a knock at the door.

There was the 11-year-old boy from next door, sobbing and saying 'Oh my mummy!'

The man rushed outside. Where there was once a house was now just a bomb crater.

The young boy's nine-year-old brother survived. So did their father, who was on duty at the gasworks. But their mother was gone.

And this was just one tragedy among *hundreds*.

The Baedeker blitz

In spring 1942 the Royal Air Force bombed the historic German town of Lubeck.

In retaliation the Nazis announced they would attack historic British towns and cities singled out for praise in the pre-war Baedeker travel guides: Bath, Canterbury, Exeter, York - and Norwich.

On the nights of April 27-28 and April 29-30, a total of almost 70 bombers attacked Norwich. No-one who was there will ever forget those nights. The devastation was terrible.

Over the two nights an estimated 240 **tons** of high explosive and fire bombs rained down on Norwich.

The poor city folk didn't stand a chance.

The first night saw 162 killed and more than 600 injured, with the area around Oak Street, City Station (what is now the Halford's roundabout on the ring road) and Dereham Road particularly badly hit.

Whole streets were flattened.

One bomb landed in Chapelfield Gardens, right on top of an air raid shelter - with terrible results.

It was East Anglia's worst air raid of the war.

The second night saw 69 more people killed and 89 injured. Firebombs caused huge damage in the city centre.

The only reason fewer people died on the second raid was that tens of thousands had fled into the countryside.

Altogether more than 7000 homes and seven churches were destroyed or damaged in the attacks.

Once again, there were some incredible stories of bravery.

John Grix, a 15-year-old boy, was blown off his bike **FIVE** times by bomb blasts - but got straight back on each time and pedalled off to deliver vital messages.

Despite the horror, people stayed amazingly cheerful.

In May, Eastern Regional Commander Sir Will Spens said: 'I think Norwich has 'taken it' marvellously. I have talked to lots of people in the streets, in rest centres and in factories and I have not heard a single whine.'

One story which shows this was the two window cleaners, with their barrows and ladders, who stood looking at the hundreds of shattered windows after one raid. 'Hey bor!,' they shouted to someone selling papers in the street, 'Can you find us a job hawking [selling] newspapers instead!'

'I'm shattered – and so is my career'

Still the raids went on. On June 26-27 up to 20,000 fire bombs rained down on Norwich, causing huge property damage but, luckily, relatively few casualties.

The Cathedral was hit in the attack, but the fires were put out in time.

After Baedecker came... butterflies.

Butterflies with a sting

These weren't the cute coloured fluttery sort. These were 2kg mini-bombs, dropped in their thousands.

They may have been small, but they would explode at the slightest touch.

It was easy to trip over them in fields and in the streets - with deadly results. It was another headache for the UXB crews.

Raids began to ease off as British and American air crews gained mastery of the skies.

But the Nazis had one more nasty trick up their sleeves...

V-ery nasty

In September 1944 the Germans fired their deadliest secret weapons at London and Norwich. The weapon was the V2 rocket.

Because it flew faster than the speed of sound, the earliest people knew that it was coming was - when it hit.

Luckily, although it was fast it wasn't very accurate.

Almost 50 were aimed at Norwich, but the nearest they got was one exploding on Hellesdon golf course - but the huge explosion and damage to 500 homes nearby showed just how lucky Norwich was.

Counting the cost

Norwich paid a terrible price for being close to the German airfields.

There were 46 air raids in total, leaving around 400 people dead and injuring more than 7000 others. An amazing 30,000 homes were damaged. Eight out of the city's famous 39 churches were destroyed or damaged.

So the nastiest nastiness in Norwich's history was saved until last.

Planning for the future
But it was a tribute to the people of Norwich that the devastation gave them the chance to redesign the city.

The inner and outer ring roads were built. New estates, schools, shops went up. The old industries like boot and shoe making faded - but new firms moved in instead.

At the start of the 21st century Norwich is still a Fine City. It's had a nasty past, as we've seen, but as for the future we have a feeling that it's going to stay...

NICE NORWICH!

Meet the team

TREVOR HEATON is the author or editor of several books on Norfolk. His last project was a big, heavy one for grown-ups so he decided to do a small, fun one for kids! He studied archaeology at school and university, and is a journalist for the Eastern Daily Press. He was actually born in King's Lynn, not Norwich, but won't tell anyone if you don't!

HOLLY JAMES lives and works in Norwich. Having studied Graphic Design at college she now works full time for a local Architectural Practice within the Graphics Department. Holly enjoys spending any free time drawing and illustrating for books just like 'Nasty Norwich' (which is much more fun!).